PREFACE

WHEN our senior pastor, R. Kent Hughes, retired from College Church in Wheaton, Illinois, after twenty-seven years of exemplary leadership, I was asked to take the position of nonpreaching interim pastor. Since the other nine pastors on staff were relatively young, Dr. Hughes and the elders thought it would be helpful both to the congregation and to the staff for an older, more seasoned pastor to be there for the congregants. It had been many years since I had been an undershepherd, but I was honored to step in. Two of my assignments were to visit the parishioners and to write and deliver the pastoral prayer each Sunday morning.

I had grown up in a church that only believed in extemporaneous prayers; indeed, spontaneity was considered *more spiritual* than carefully prepared prayers. But as I matured in my faith and studied the prayers preserved throughout Christian history, I discovered the richness and depth of prayer that teaches and elevates the hearers. I gravitated to the words of Puritan pastors who combined the teaching of God's Word with presenting the needs of their people to God.

As I visited our parishioners month after month, it became abundantly clear that many of them were privately struggling with life's common issues: unemployment, deteriorating health, financial crisis, family disruption, wrenching loss, seemingly unanswered prayer. The list included every kind of human frailty. Their hearts cried out to me and to God. When I sat down to write my pastoral prayer each week, I tried to express their feelings, voice their concerns, and ask their questions. The prayers in this book are the result.

Following the Puritans' example, I drew inspiration from the heartfelt needs of God's people in my own church, but I also have drawn from scriptural phrases and passages as well as words from hymns. Sometimes I quote a Scripture verse directly; in other cases, I adapt it slightly. As you read through the prayers, these words from the Bible and other sources are set in italics and the respective sources are included at the end of each prayer.

The number of prayers for each month varies; sometimes there are more or fewer prayers than there are Sundays in a month. Rather than presenting a designated week-by-week selection, I've offered a collection of prayers from over the years for your discretionary use. Some prayers commemorate particular events that are either on the church-year calendar or the secular calendar, but the majority of the prayers were written as expressions of personal praise and petition. Almost every week someone would ask me for a copy of the Sunday prayer to share with a friend or loved one. I am grateful to know that some of these prayers have been sent around the world or reprinted in various publications.

I gratefully acknowledge Pauline Epps, who successfully deciphered and typed my handwritten notes, and Beth Bergman, who shaped the spoken words into a more readable form.

WENDELL C. HAWLEY

A
Pastor Prays
for His People

A Collection of Wise and Loving Prayers
to Help You through Life's Journey

WENDELL C. HAWLEY

Tyndale House Publishers, Inc.
CAROL STREAM, ILLINOIS

Visit Tyndale's exciting Web site at www.tyndale.com.

TYNDALE and Tyndale's quill logo are registered trademarks of Tyndale House Publishers, Inc.

A Pastor Prays for His People: A Collection of Wise and Loving Prayers to Help You through Life's Journey

Copyright © 2010 by Wendell C. Hawley. All rights reserved.

Cover red background pattern copyright © by Selahattin Bayram/iStockphoto. All rights reserved.

Cover gold background pattern copyright © by Ashwin Kharidehal Abhirama/iStockphoto. All rights reserved.

Cover illustration of church copyright © by Christain Tölg/iStockphoto. All rights reserved.

Author photo copyright © April 2009 by Sean Shimmel at TimeStandStillStudio.com. All rights reserved.

Designed by Ron Kaufmann

Edited by Bonne Steffen

All Scripture quotations, unless otherwise indicated, are taken from the New King James Version.®
Copyright © 1982 by Thomas Nelson, Inc. Used by permission. All rights reserved.

Scripture quotations marked NLT are taken from the Holy Bible, New Living Translation, second edition,
copyright © 1996, 2004, 2007 by Tyndale House Foundation. (Some quotations may be from the NLT, first
edition, copyright © 1996.) Used by permission of Tyndale House Publishers, Inc., Carol Stream, Illinois
60188. All rights reserved.

Scripture quotations marked KJV are taken from the Holy Bible, King James Version.

Scripture quotations marked NIV are taken from the Holy Bible, New International Version,® NIV.® Copyright
© 1973, 1978, 1984 by Biblica, Inc.™ Used by permission of Zondervan. All rights reserved worldwide.
www.zondervan.com.

Scripture quotations marked NASB are taken from the New American Standard Bible,® copyright © 1960,
1962, 1963, 1968, 1971, 1972, 1973, 1975, 1977, 1995 by The Lockman Foundation. Used by permission.

Scripture quotations marked RSV are taken from the Revised Standard Version of the Bible, copyright ©
1952 [2nd edition, 1971] by the Division of Christian Education of the National Council of the Churches of
Christ in the United States of America. Used by permission. All rights reserved.

Library of Congress Cataloging-in-Publication Data

Hawley, Wendell C., date.
    A pastor prays for his people : a collection of wise and loving prayers to help you through life's journey /
Wendell C. Hawley.
        p. cm.
    Includes index.
    ISBN 978-1-4143-3908-5 (sc)
    1. Pastoral prayers. I. Title.
BV250.H39 2010
264′.13—dc22   2010022910

Printed in the United States of America

16   15   14   13   12   11   10
7   6   5   4   3   2   1

JANUARY

Talking to men for God is a great thing,
but talking to God for men is greater still!

E. M. BOUNDS

Gracious God, eternal Father,
Maker and master of all things,
We praise you that with endless bounty you have made provision for **every**
    need experienced by your children.
We rejoice as we contemplate the truth
    that not one solitary need among us today
    finds you indifferent or helpless or catches you by surprise.
No one but our God could say:
    "Before you call, I will answer."
We are staggered by such divine munificence.

Help us to really believe that
    you know,
    you care,
    you will answer.
Now in this moment, all who come to the house of worship with a heavy
    burden are going to leave it with you.

{ SILENT PRAYER }

O Lord, we praise you for a faith that teaches us
    to sing,
    to pray,
    and to hope.

To **sing** . . .
Others from yesteryear's household of faith honored God while facing
    overwhelming circumstances.

3

They sang of the *wonderful goodness* of the Lord.
Moses, Deborah, David, and Mary teach us
    to sing—when being tested;
    to sing—when sorrow has us in its grip;
    to sing—when we don't feel like it;
    to sing—*a new song*
        when we've passed through a crisis;
        when we've had a fresh experience of God's provision;
        when we've been given *songs in the night.*
Someday we shall join Moses and the hosts of heaven in singing:
    "Great and marvelous are your works,
    Lord God Almighty!
    Just and true are your ways."

We praise you for a faith that teaches us to **pray**.
    Not endless repetitions,
    not mindless mantras,
    not magical incantations,
    not with ringing of bells and clapping of hands,
    not in a catatonic stupor.
Rather, as a redeemed soul in fellowship with the Redeemer.
    So, like the disciples, we say, *Lord, teach us to pray.*

We praise you for a faith that teaches us to **hope**.
    Hope is our anchor in the storms and stresses of life.
        We hope in God.
        We have a *blessed hope.*
        We have the *confident hope of heaven.*
Your promises, Father God, are sure and reliable—
    that gives us hope.

        ✦ Amen.

Isaiah 65:24; Psalm 145:7, NLT; Psalm 149:1; Job 35:10; Revelation 15:3;
Luke 11:1; Titus 2:13; Colossians 1:5, NLT

God of all grace, God of my salvation,
I praise you because you are *the same yesterday, today, and forever.*
You never grow old; you are not impoverished, enfeebled, forgetful;
  your *faithfulness continues to each generation—*
    more enduring than the earth itself.
And yet, wonder of wonders, you have entered into our existence,
for the eternal *Word became flesh and dwelt among us.*
And because of that, Jesus knows all about life's struggles.

We thank you, Father God, that Jesus had to earn a living.
  He did a day's work like any working person;
  he had to face the wearying routine of everyday work,
    work that sometimes becomes a chore . . . a struggle.
He knew the frustration and irritation of serving the public . . .
  some people are never pleased.
Jesus knew the problems of living together in a family.
He knew what it was like to have unbelieving relatives.
And he knew the reality of temptation and the attacks of Satan.

We thank you, Father God, that Jesus shared in happy social
    occasions . . .
  that he was at ease at weddings, and at dinner parties,
  and at festivals in the homes of the rich and the poor . . .
    and people just like us.
Grant, Father, that we may ever remember that in his unseen, risen presence,

he is a guest in our homes and a listener to every conversation.
We thank you that Jesus knew the meaning of friendship,
that he had his own circle of friends with whom he wanted to be;
that he knew how to catch fish and how to prepare a meal;
and that he was there, standing alongside loved ones, when they
needed him most.

He also knew what it was like to be disappointed by a friend,
to suffer disloyalty,
to have love repaid by rejection.
He experienced unfair criticism,
prejudiced opposition,
deliberate misunderstanding.
He was lied about and abandoned—he knew what it was like
to be alone.
We thank you, Father, that whatever circumstances we face,
Jesus has been there before.
Because *he faced all of the same testings we do,*
he is able to help those who are going through them.
Touched with the feeling of our infirmities, *he knows our frame;*
he remembers that we are dust.
Therefore, we come boldly to the throne of grace,
that we may obtain mercy and find grace to help in every time of need.

Lord, we are a needy people . . . in need of your assurances.
As we hide your Word away in our hearts,
make every promise real to us this year.
Great peace have those who love your law, and nothing causes them to stumble.

And so, sovereign Lord, as we face the New Year,
we do so in the confidence that you are with us in the midst of every
situation:
sickness or health;

empty purses or stretched dollars;
business losses or economic gains;
family disruption or family delights.
Whatever, Lord, we are yours!

✝ *Amen.*

Hebrews 13:8; Psalm 100:5, NLT; John 1:14; Hebrews 4:15, NLT; Hebrews 4:15, KJV;
Psalm 103:14; Hebrews 4:16; Psalm 119:165

Our Father and our God,
You are eternal; as for us, *our days are numbered.*
Seasons and years come and go, but they do not diminish you one iota;
    meanwhile we are very much aware of what the march of time
        does to us.
You, O Lord, are *the same yesterday, today, and forever.*
We begin life's journey thinking that we are invincible,
    only to find out we are very fragile.
You are the **source** of all life; every breath we take is a gift from you.

We learn from your eternal Word of our destitute condition, and we praise
    you for permission
    to approach your *throne of grace.*
We give thanks for your matchless condescension,
    that we fallen creatures, desperately in need of reconciliation,
    may experience the imputed righteousness of Christ, our Savior.
Your gracious announcement to us is:
    "The one who comes to me I will by no means cast out."
With that assurance ringing in our hearts, we come boldly to the mercy seat
    and spread our desires and needs before you.
    Cleanse our hearts,
    remove our iniquities,
    soothe our hurts,
    establish our steps,
    take away our fears,

lift our burdens,
and may we see your work of saving grace among our loved ones.
Tune our hearts to anticipate with great joy the awesome cry,
    "Behold, the bridegroom is coming!"

Give shelter to the homeless,
    food to the hungry,
    work to the unemployed,
    care and assistance to the needy,
    comfort to those who mourn.
Give us receptive hearts to the message from your Word today.

✝ Amen.

Psalm 39:4, NLT; Hebrews 13:8; Hebrews 4:16; John 6:37; Matthew 25:6

Our Father and our God, God of our heart's desire,
We fail in our attempts to adequately describe you.
We marshal all the adjectives of adoration we can think of,
    and when we have exhausted our vocabulary,
    we have not begun to encompass you.
Blessed Redeemer, Sweet Rose of Sharon, Balm in Gilead,
    we worship you and praise you for revealing yourself, even in part,
        to us, your creatures;
        to us, your children.

Father, since last we entered this place of worship, a shadow has crossed
    our pathway.
We wanted only sunshine . . . but experienced a chill.
The enemy of our souls cast doubts by saying:
    "Has God said?"
    "Those promises are not for you."
    And in that hour our trust wavered.
Merciful God, strengthen our faith and trust in you,
    for we are *the sheep of your pasture;*
        we need our Shepherd's presence.
Thanks be to God! He gives us the victory through our Lord Jesus Christ,
    and we are made overcomers by the blood of the Lamb.

God of compassion, as you look upon your children around the world,
    many are suffering.

We pray that you will
   deliver the oppressed,
   encourage the seemingly insignificant,
   raise the fallen,
   provide for the needy,
   heal the sick,
   bring back those who have gone astray.
Make wars to cease and every nation come to know that
   you alone are God and that
   your Son, Jesus Christ, provides plenteous redemption.
Today, wherever the gospel is preached,
   when the Good News is declared,
   may your people rejoice and may many others come to faith.

And now we pray the prayer guide you gave the disciples:
Our Father which art in heaven,
hallowed be thy name.
Thy kingdom come,
thy will be done in earth,
   as it is in heaven.
Give us this day our daily bread.
And forgive us our debts,
   as we forgive our debtors.
And lead us not into temptation,
   but deliver us from evil.
For thine is the kingdom, and the power, and the glory, for ever.

✢ Amen.

Genesis 3:1; Psalm 79:13; 1 Corinthians 15:57, NIV; 2 Kings 19:19, NLT; Matthew 6:9-13, KJV

Gracious God, Comforter of all who put their trust in you,
We acknowledge that our trust is wavering.
So many stressful things are happening:
    health issues . . . life is so fragile;
    financial pressures . . . loved ones are dependent on me;
    family situations . . . bad decisions have led to bad attitudes.
Lord, like David, I need to *tell you all my troubles.*
    I feel battered, pummeled, overwhelmed, helpless—
        fearful in the midst of my circumstances.
My vision is limited to this day . . .
I can't see over or around or through or beyond my circumstances.
    In such a time as this, David said:
        "God is our refuge."

Refuge . . .
God is my shelter, protection,
    safety, security, anchorage,
    resource, seclusion, aid,
    defense, support, guardianship,
    haven, fortress, provision,
    harbor, sanctum.
When I consider what you are, I echo the poet:
    Other refuge have I none;
        Hangs my helpless soul on thee.

Leave, ah, leave me not alone,
Still support and comfort me.

Lord, your eternal Word assures me that you are *a very present help*,
not a distant help,
not a begrudging help,
not a delaying help,
not an inadequate help,
not an illusory nor a fickle help . . .
but a prevalent, substantial, immediate, efficacious, powerful help in time
of need.
Now, in your house, in your presence,
each of us confess our sins,
confess our needs,
confess our utter trust in you.

{ SILENT PRAYER }

Thank you, Father God. With renewed vigor, we refresh our souls by the
words of Scripture:
The Lord will work out his plans for my life.
They will see in our history the faithful love of the Lord.
Great Shepherd, make this true:
that our children, grandchildren, neighbors, friends,
extended family, unbelievers, coworkers . . .
Everyone who has eyes to see and ears to hear will know . . . **God is faithful!**
Praise his name forever!

✢ *Amen.*

Psalm 142:2, NLT; Psalm 46:1; Charles Wesley, "Jesus, Lover of My Soul"; Psalm 46:1;
Psalm 138:8, NLT; Psalm 107:43, NLT; Isaiah 32:3, NLT

Almighty God, holy God,
We approach your throne as did Solomon of long ago, acknowledging,
there is no God like you in all of heaven or earth.
You are more holy than we can imagine:
so pure, unregenerate eyes will never see you,
so powerful, no force on earth can thwart your sovereign will.
Ah, but so gracious, none are turned away who earnestly seek you.
The heavens cannot contain you, yet you deign to be present,
where even *two or three are gathered in your name.*
Blessed be your name forever.

This is the day of worship, the day set aside because of Jesus'
resurrection.
May this hour be rich in blessings that the Lord's Day was designed
to impart,
rich in
heart-centered worship,
food from the Word,
invigorated faith,
renewed spiritual purpose.

I praise you for your *throne of grace.* . . .
by your invitation we have open access, through the blood
of Jesus Christ.
It is here we find you ready to hear our plea,

waiting to show mercy and offer grace for every need,
inviting us to pour out our confessions.
Here you promise to give *more than we can ask or think!*

This is the place . . . the hour . . . of full and free forgiveness.
So with contrite hearts we confess our times of irreverent worship,
ingratitude,
listless praise,
worldly cares,
misplaced affections.

{ SILENT PRAYER }

Forgive us, Lord. We thank you, God, for hearing our prayers
and removing our sins.

☩ *Amen.*

---

1 Kings 8:23, NLT; Matthew 18:20; Hebrews 4:16; Ephesians 3:20, NLT

FEBRUARY

Merciful God, open our eyes that we might see the fullness of Christ,
and remove the lopsided and distorted images of your Son
that weaken our worship.

JOHN PIPER

Sovereign Lord, Creator, sustainer of the universe,
Your unrivaled authority knows no boundary,
   no limitation,
   no contingency,
   no uncertainty.
Impress upon our minds the consciousness of your greatness and the
      awe-inspiring truth:
   With you *one day is as a thousand years, and a thousand years*
      as one day.
You are a mighty God who, amidst the revolutions of empires,
   experiences no variableness,
   no *shadow of turning,*
      but rather you are glorious in immortality.
We are as fading flowers, withering grass; our days are limited,
      numbered.
But you, O Lord, are the Rock of Ages.

In great condescension, you have revealed to us
   the glories of your grace,
   the power of your forgiveness,
   the certainty of your Word.
May our hearts know true repentance and all our desires be compatible with
      your will.
We confess our sins.

Now, by the enabling of the Holy Spirit, may we *live holy lives.*

As we contemplate the blessings of our salvation in Christ,
we are aware of the multitudes around us
who live in gospel ignorance.
Their lives are darkened, fearful, without hope, lost, condemned.
We pray that every effort to get the Good News to these people will be
mightily blessed by you.

We pray your mercy upon families whose children have been killed
through random shootings.
Those who deeply grieve must be in shock and despair.
May they learn of the comfort that comes from God alone and in the face
of unanswered mystery,
may those who mourn hear your voice:
"Come unto me, you who are heavy laden, and I will give you rest."

Visit in sanctifying grace those who tread deep waters,
those who grieve,
those who suffer,
those who are experiencing shattered relationships,
those who need in one way or another the touch of God in the midst
of overwhelming circumstances.
May this be an hour when our hearts rejoice in your provision.
We pray in Jesus' name.

✣ *Amen.*

---

2 Peter 3:8; James 1:17; 2 Peter 3:11, NLT; Matthew 11:28

Almighty and everlasting God,
Who *numbers the stars* in order and *turns darkness into light,*
  you have *set eternity within the heart of man.*
We think about eternity and trust in you.
Your promises are written in our hearts . . . we believe them.
  What no eye has seen, nor ear heard,
  And what has not entered into the heart of man . . .
  You have prepared for those who love you.
The credo of others may be,
  Let us eat and drink, for tomorrow we die!
But for us of the transformed heart,
  We seek a city whose builder and maker is God.

Thanks be to God . . .
You are light to the wanderer,
  joy of the pilgrim,
  refuge of the brokenhearted,
  deliverer of the oppressed,
  strength of the tempted,
  rescuer of the perishing,
  hope of the dying,
  Savior of sinners.
We long to hear that voice from heaven saying:
  "The kingdoms of this world are become the kingdoms of our Lord, and of his
    Christ, and he shall reign for ever and ever."
  Praise be unto God.

Father God, the world presses in upon us every waking hour.

We are squeezed and pulled and rudely affected by a system contrary to the
way of the Cross.

Consequently, we are shocked to realize how subtly the world's approval,
language,
conduct,
attitude
seeps into our life.

Help us remember that Vanity Fair is not our home; we are just passing
through.

We are sojourners . . . just a breath away from our eternal home.

Keep us unencumbered lest our goods become our gods, and our cares,
cankers.

And now, Father God, give ear to each penitential prayer as we ask for
forgiveness and grace.

{ SILENT PRAYER }

Thank you for clean hearts and revived spirits.

✠ *Amen.*

Psalm 147:4; Psalm 18:28, NIV; Ecclesiastes 3:11, NIV; 1 Corinthians 2:9;
Isaiah 22:13; Hebrews 11:10; Revelation 11:15, KJV

Glorious God, wonderful Savior,
We turn to you, believing that you are more ready to hear than we are
 inclined to pray.
Your invitation to us holds no exclusions.
You have not limited our access to your presence to certain hours,
 certain days, certain circumstances.
The apostle Peter assures us that God watches over his people and
 he hears their prayers.
Lord, we believe this to be true, and yet we are appalled at our neglect.
Facing overwhelming difficulties and reacting in desperation,
 we have turned elsewhere in our need:
  to friends, teachers, lawyers, government . . .
We've talked to anyone, anywhere, that we think might solve our
 problems.
All the while your Word should get our attention:
 No good thing will God withhold from them that walk uprightly.

Lord, you are the best judge of what is good for us.
Forgive us for not believing this and help us to grasp this truth today.
Help each of us to pray:
 "Lord, I want what you will give, and I don't want what you would
  withhold."
May all our wants be captured by that grid.

We are confident that you want to cleanse us of sin, giving us victory over
 evil habits,

wrong attitudes,
bad tempers,
lustful desires.
And with these removed, you will give us
trust,
patience,
calmness
as we wait upon you.

By your Holy Spirit help us to *walk uprightly*
before our families, our coworkers, our neighbors, the watching world.
May there not be in us any crooked dealings:
no dishonesty, no hypocrisy, no deceit.
The walk of uprightness is the way of **heavenly wealth—**
wealth so large as to include *every good thing.*
May we *hunger and thirst for righteousness.*
May we *walk uprightly and receive "good things" from the Lord* today.

✝ *Amen.*

---

1 Peter 3:12; Psalm 84:11; Isaiah 57:2; Psalm 84:11; Matthew 5:6; Psalm 84:11

Lord of power, Lord of grace,
All hearts are in your hands, all events are of your sovereign will.
    You alone do all things well.
Sometimes we don't think all is well.
We pray for the change of hearts in others,
    but maybe it is our own hearts that need your transforming power!
Perhaps the failures we condemn in others are really our own failures.
Perhaps situations are distorted because of the *log in our own eye*
    even as we complain about the speck in another's eye.

If this be the case, help us to focus on what you want to teach us . . .
    the changes needed in our hearts.
Convicted by your Holy Spirit,
    enlightened by your holy Word,
    enabled by your powerful presence,
    assured by your matchless grace,
I confess my sins, my failures, my foolish independence, my lovelessness,
believing that
    If we confess our sins, you are faithful and just to forgive us our sins and
        cleanse us from all unrighteousness.
    Thank you, God, for complete forgiveness.

Now I pray honestly and earnestly, God of great power: Control my tongue.
    Keep me from saying things that make trouble;
    from involving myself in arguments

that only make bad situations worse,
only cause further alienation,
· and make me think everyone else is at fault except me.
Control my thoughts.
Shut the door of my mind against all envious and jealous thoughts.
Shut the door of my mind against all bitter and resentful thoughts.
Shut the door of my mind against all ugly and unclean thoughts.
Help me to live in purity and in love.
Henceforth, may my focus be on the completion of your work—your good
work—in my soul.
Then, Good Shepherd, *I shall not be ashamed on the day of Jesus Christ.*

Lord, bless the proclamation of your Word today, around the world.
May many have ears to hear the Good News of salvation.

✢ Amen.

Matthew 7:5, NLT; 1 John 1:9; 2 Timothy 1:12

MARCH

My desire is to be so filled with the Word and the needs of my people

that as I pray we are all borne up to God.

R. KENT HUGHES

Almighty God, governor of the universe,
Judge of all men, head of the church, Savior of sinners—
    your greatness is unsearchable . . .
    your goodness, infinite . . .
    your compassions, unfailing . . .
    your providence, boundless . . .
        your mercies, ever new.

We praise you for the invitation to salvation, the gospel of peace.
Your Son is our **only** refuge, our **only** hope, our **only** confidence.
We are weak, but Jesus is mighty.
Nothing we face stretches you.
    No predicament . . .
    No loss . . .
    No need . . . but what *you are able to do exceeding abundantly above all that*
        we ask or think.
Knowing—trusting in such divine provision—we fear no more.
Hear now our confessions.

{ SILENT PRAYER }

Having confessed our sins, we do believe
    you have forgiven our sins and cleansed us from all unrighteousness.
May our consciences be clear,
    our hearts pure;

our sleep refreshing;
   and may no evil befall us.
Sovereign Lord, we pray particularly for the Muslim world.
Its needs are staggering, its spiritual darkness impenetrable, apart from the
   light of the gospel of the Lord Jesus Christ.
We ask you to bless every endeavor to make Christ known to Muslims.
May millions from Muslim countries be a part
   of that great and glorious number
   from *every tribe, every tongue, every nation,*
      who will make up the eternal Kingdom of God.

Remember in mercy the needs of this congregation.
   Heal the sick,
   succor the tempted,
   strengthen the weary,
   guide the confused,
   lift up the fallen,
   supply the needy,
   convict the sinner,
   teach the ignorant,
   comfort the grieving.
And after quickening us by your Word today, send us *on our way rejoicing.*

✢ *Amen.*

Lamentations 3:22; Lamentations 3:23, NLT; Ephesians 3:20; 1 John 1:9;
Revelation 14:6; Acts 8:39

God of glory, God of grace,
It is only by the invitation of your Son, our blessed Redeemer, that we
approach the place of mercy.
We come *boldly unto the throne of grace, that we may obtain mercy and find
grace in time of need.*
Lord, **you know** how needy we are.
Before others, we mask our needs . . .
We say "all is well" and continue our bravado, hoping our facade will not
betray our real situation.
Forgive us for such deception.
We confess our stubborn insistence on running our own lives, telling
ourselves that we are really pretty good and that we are quite
successful—
But then, the light of your holy Word shines in our hearts and we see the
reality of our condition.

"I am a man of unclean lips," cried Isaiah.
"My sin is ever before me," prayed David.
"I am a sinful man," said Simon Peter.
And Saul of Tarsus would confess that he was *the chief of sinners*—
But each of these men found that *where sin abounded, grace did much
more abound!*
That's why we come to you . . . we need **boundless** grace,
grace that meets every need,
grace that is more than sufficient . . .

for broken relationships,
broken hearts,
broken promises.
Now as we each pray personally, forgive, strengthen, and stabilize your
people.

{ SILENT PRAYER }

Thank you, faithful Father.
Fulfill in our lives today what the apostle Paul prayed for the Thessalonians:
May our Lord Jesus Christ and God our Father,
who loved us and in his special favor gave us everlasting comfort and good hope,
comfort our hearts and give us strength in every good thing we do and say.

✠ 𝔄men.

Hebrews 4:16; Isaiah 6:5; Psalm 51:3, KJV; Luke 5:8; 1 Timothy 1:15;
Romans 5:20, KJV; 2 Thessalonians 2:16-17

God of hope, God of mercy,
Faithful God, forgiving God, holy God,
We have your Word, your promise—and we trust in the fact that
the Lord is near to all who call upon him,
to all who call upon him in truth.
We have been invited *to ask, to seek, to knock,* with promise of answer,
for we believe you rule over all,
and in your hand is power and might.
So we address our petitions to
the King eternal, immortal, invisible, the only God, worthy to receive honor
and glory for ever and ever.

Father God, we would that our moments of trust were with us always,
but events come into our lives and we are filled with questions.
We need the reinforcement that you have the answers.
We stand mute before inexplicable circumstances, but there are no
mysteries for you.
There are no facts you do not know;
no problems you cannot solve;
no events you cannot explain;
no hypocrisy through which you do not see;
no secrets of ours unknown to you.

We are truly unmasked before you, and you see us as we really are—
filled with our pride,

our selfishness,
our shallowness,
our impatience,
    our blatant carnality.
We would despair were it not so that
    you, O Lord, are compassionate and gracious,
    slow to anger and abounding in loving-kindness. . . .
You have not dealt with us according to our sins,
    for as high as the heavens are above the earth,
    so great is your loving-kindness toward those who fear you.

So we crave today
    a clean life,
    a quiet spirit,
    an honest tongue,
    a believing heart,
    a redeemed soul.
Thank you, God, that the blood of Jesus Christ *cleanses us from*
    all unrighteousness.
Now, may we enjoy you forever!

✝ 𝔄men.

Psalm 145:18; Matthew 7:7; 1 Timothy 1:17, KJV; Hebrews 4:13;
Psalm 103:8, 10-11, NASB; 1 John 1:9

Palm Sunday Prayer

Christ our God, Prince of Peace,
Who on this day did enter the rebellious city *midst shouts of "Hosanna,"*
  enter our hearts and subdue them entirely unto you.
Rule over us in all the concerns and circumstances of our lives:
  the work of our hands and the whims of our hearts;
  the ambitions of our dreams and the sins of our desires;
  the experience of our friendships and our secret thoughts toward others.

Save us from the hypocrisy that sings "Hosanna" in the temple and cries
  "Crucify him" in the marketplace of daily business.
Save us from the sham that praises with the lips, but betrays you in our
  deeds.
Save us from the treason that boasts loyalty in the upper room and then
  makes cowardly denial in the judgment hall.

Lord, grant that as you look over us this moment,
  you will not weep as you did riding into Jerusalem on that momentous day.
Grant that every person in this place of worship will want you as king of
  their lives,
  as sovereign monarch in every relationship.
May each of us in reverence and adoration truly say,
  "Hosanna in the highest! Blessed is he who comes in the name of the Lord!"

We pray that the day will speedily arrive when, at your glorious return,
  every knee shall bow, and every tongue confess
  that you are Lord, to the glory of God the Father.

We pray this as we pray the prayer you taught the disciples:
Our Father which art in heaven,
hallowed be thy name.
Thy kingdom come,
thy will be done in earth,
    as it is in heaven.
Give us this day our daily bread.
And forgive us our debts,
    as we forgive our debtors.
And lead us not into temptation,
    but deliver us from evil.
For thine is the kingdom, and the power, and the glory, for ever.

✝ ᴀmen.

Mark 11:9; Luke 19:41; Mark 11:9-10; Philippians 2:10-11; Matthew 6:9-13, KJV

Easter Prayer

Ever-living and glorious God,
Triumphant and sovereign Savior,
we worship you, Lord of the universe,
  Creator of life physical,
  Source of life eternal.
Enable us to adequately praise you.
Just as our love for our family is expressed **joyfully,**
  we **joyfully** praise you for our salvation—indeed, a great salvation.

A million cemeteries dot the face of the earth, and only one is different—
  only one contains a vacated tomb.
Guards, seals, soldiers . . .
  all the hosts of death and destruction could not restrict the Lord of Glory.
The resurrected Christ—the one who came to seek and save those who
    were lost—
  now provides the way to reconciliation with a holy God.
Because the grave could not hold Jesus, we know it will not hold those
    who belong to him.
  This is our certainty!
    For this we joyfully praise God.
Living Savior, substantially comfort the grieving members of our flock
    and others experiencing difficult days—
  dark, shadowy days,
  days when the gloom of "Friday" seems more persistent than the
    brightness of Sunday.

These despondent ones need the *Emmaus Road experience*—
a transformation only a risen Savior can give.
So while we pray, transform troubled hearts into joy-filled hearts,
hearts captivated by
a risen, victorious, eternal Savior.
All this we pray in the name which is above all other names,
the name of Jesus,
our only hope,
our only Savior.

✣ Amen.

Luke 24:13-32

Easter Prayer

Holy and ever-living God,
Who has *set eternity in the heart of man,*
enable us to adequately praise you for *shattering the power of death.*
Our emotions are deeply stirred by the joy of the Resurrection—
  a resurrection that turned mankind's night into light and our mourning
  into laughter.

We praise you for the victory that turned the cross from a symbol
  of shame to a symbol of triumph,
  the ultimate expression of love.
We resonate with the hymn writer:
  Oh, the cross has wondrous glory!
    Oft I've proved this to be true;
  When I'm in the way so narrow,
    I can see a pathway through.
Living Savior, fill with fresh hope and consolation every heart present
  who has lost earth's dearest treasure.
Make every life—overcome with the sense of loss—be radiant today
  because of the truth of the Resurrection.
Our gospel is "Good News," and the Good News is:
  Christ died for our sins according to the Scriptures,
  and that he was buried,
  and that he rose again the third day according to the Scriptures.

Mighty God, we thank you for the Victory of Easter—
  the grave is not the end.

Loving God, we thank you for the Peace of Easter—
the atonement for our sins has been made.
Eternal God, we thank you for the Hope of Easter—
because Christ lives, we shall live also.

✝ *Amen.*

Ecclesiastes 3:11, NIV; Hebrews 2:14; William Hunter, "Is Not This the Land of Beulah?"; 1 Corinthians 15:3-4; John 14:19

APRIL

I am praying for them. I am not praying for the world,
but for these whom you have given me, for they are yours.

JESUS

Almighty and merciful God,
You have always been the provider and protector of your people.
No circumstance of our doing can limit your divine purpose.
Against great odds, you led the Israelites across the Red Sea.
With you, O Lord, there is no *"Red Sea"* we cannot cross;
  there is no *lions' den* where we cannot be safe.
  There is no *fiery furnace* but that you are with us;
  no battlefield but what *guarding angels* may be a protecting shield.

So we praise you this hour for a fresh realization that
  if God be for us, who can be against us?
We praise you, Father, for your steadfast protection of our very own
    military participants.
You have brought safely back to us, to family and dear ones,

_____.

They join many others in this congregation whom you have protected
    in time of war and brought safely home.
May the rest of us, in the battlefield of life, be divinely protected from all
    the subtleties,
  from all the maliciousness,
  from all the destruction of the evil one.
We ask, Lord Jesus, that you guard and garrison us,
  for *we know not what a day will bring forth.*
    Perhaps sickness, loss, separation, disappointment—
      in every situation, may the grace of God be abundant and sufficient.

And now may we pray from our hearts the prayer you taught the disciples:
Our Father which art in heaven,
hallowed be thy name.
Thy kingdom come,
thy will be done in earth,
   as it is in heaven.
Give us this day our daily bread.
And forgive us our debts,
   as we forgive our debtors.
And lead us not into temptation,
   but deliver us from evil.
For thine is the kingdom, and the power, and the glory, for ever.

✝ *A*men.

Exodus 14; Daniel 6; Daniel 3; Psalm 91:11; Romans 8:31, KJV; James 4:14;
Matthew 6:9-13, KJV

Almighty God, Creator, giver of life,
We bless your holy name for such gifts.
We are dependent upon you for each breath we take—
    whether we enjoy the zest of youth or bear the frailties of old age,
        we exist by your mercies.
Should you withdraw your providential hand from us, we would
    cease to be.
    Your greatness is beyond our comprehension!
Before you, nations rise and fall, generations come and go—
    you alone are unchanging, unwavering, everlasting—
    you are God.

We, whose times are in your hands, we worship you.
Great and marvelous are your works, O Lord God.
    Righteous and true are your ways, King of Glory.
Overawed by your greatness, we join the millions of angels saying,
    "Holy, holy, holy, Lord God of hosts,
    the heaven of heavens cannot contain you."

And yet, you love us who once were your enemies—
    captured, as it were, by sin,
    blinded by unbelief,
    selfish in outlook,
    disinterested and unresponsive to the claims of Christ.
While we were yet sinners, Christ died for the ungodly.

We are enveloped in your love.
It enshrouds our life, our future, our hope.
We affirm our adoration, praying:
Bless the Lord, O my soul;
and all that is within me, bless his holy name! . . .
Joyful, joyful, we adore thee, God of glory, Lord of love.
So whatever it is you are doing in our lives,
however difficult the circumstances,
however painful the condition,
however puzzling the situation,
we believe you do all things well—
help us in our unbelief.

Our nation faces many challenges today; we need to remember your words:
Righteousness exalts a nation, but sin is a disgrace to any people.
May you give a desire to our leaders to lead this nation in the ways of
justice,
honesty,
integrity,
sanctity of life,
judicial uprightness.
May we truly be a beacon to the whole world.
We pray earnestly, Father, that you will incline this nation to
hunger and thirst for righteousness.
Reverse what appears to many of us to be the alarming moral descent
of our country.
Wherever the gospel is declared today, may it bring forth fruit.
We who profess to know you repent of our sins.
Revive us—revive us!

✢ *Amen.*

Isaiah 6:3; 2 Chronicles 6:18; Romans 5:6, 8; Psalm 103:1; Henry Van Dyke,
"Joyful, Joyful, We Adore Thee"; Mark 9:24; Proverbs 14:34, NIV; Matthew 5:6

Blessed God, gracious God, merciful God,
How can we express the honors of your name?
In Christ, there is
   strength for the weak,
   riches for the needy,
   wisdom for the ignorant,
   fullness for the empty,
   food for the hungry,
   raiment for those who lack,
   forgiveness for the repentant.
All this we have in your Son, our Savior, the Lord Jesus Christ.
Blessed be his name forever.

Father God, we remember the testimony of our parents, who trusted you
     in difficult times—
days far more difficult than these.
They trusted in you, believing your promises, and you delivered them.
   You provided food when the cupboard was bare;
   you provided employment when jobs were hard to find;
   you provided healing in times of great stress—
     they found *streams in the desert,*
     durable shoes in the wilderness.
For you are a trustworthy God, and when we have trusted in you, we have
     not been disappointed.
   Forgive us for our immature impatience.

King Saul couldn't wait for God to respond and took things into his hands,
  to his own great detriment.
Many others could not trust and wait upon God to answer prayers and
  provide—
  we do not want to be like them!
  Grant us faith—faith to trust you, no matter how long.
We would be like *Simeon and Anna*, who waited a lifetime but kept
  worshiping, believing, trusting that the God who promises, keeps
  his word:
  "I will never leave you nor forsake you."
Gracious God, bring us into your presence and fill us with your Holy Spirit.
Make us continually aware of your presence—even when you seem far off.
Give us the character of those who are always near you.
Give us the radiance of holiness,
  the joy of holiness,
  the peace of holiness,
  the beauty of holiness,
That we, at the apostle Peter's urging, might be *partakers of the divine nature*.

✢ Amen.

Isaiah 35:6; Deuteronomy 29:5; Luke 2:25-38; Joshua 1:5, NIV; 2 Peter 1:4

Almighty God, our Father,
We approach you with the deepest reverence—with holy boldness.
We do this because your house should be
   called a place of prayer for all nations
   and you have **invited** us to come to the *throne of grace*. We thank you.
We pray, not to inform you, for you know all things perfectly.
We pray, not to change your purposes, for you alone do all things well.
We pray because we are entirely dependent upon you
   for life, health, comfort,
   protection in the storms of life,
      and strength to wisely face the pressures of life.

I pray that you will preserve us, each one, from a foolish act by which
      others stumble,
   that your name be not blasphemed,
   that your people be not grieved,
   that the unredeemed be not further hardened,
   that none of us be found to be a hypocrite on Judgment Day.

Show us what sins hide your face from us, eclipsing your love.
We confess our open and secret sins even now as your blessed Holy Spirit
      confronts us.

{ SILENT PRAYER }

Thank you for your pardoning, healing, cleansing grace.
Repentant and forgiven, we endeavor by your help to walk with care
in the *paths of righteousness*.

Lord, you know that locked in the hearts of many here today are
fears,
hurts,
unanswered questions,
unmet needs—
burdens that are heavy to bear.
You know each situation, and as we now *cast all our cares upon you*,
may we experience enabling grace.
Comfort the grieving, particularly those who mourn most deeply.
May your grace rest in great measure upon them.
Sustain those who are ill and those who care for them.
Bless the efforts of all who are doing good for the needy.

We join the psalmist in praising you:
Your righteousness, O God, reaches to the highest heavens.
You have done such wonderful things.
You have allowed me to suffer much hardship,
but you will restore me to life again.

✢ 𝔄men.

Mark 11:17; Hebrews 4:16; Psalm 23:3; Psalm 55:22, NIV; Psalm 71:19-20, NLT

Most gracious God,
You have promised mercy through Jesus Christ to all who repent and
    believe in him.
We know that our only salvation is in Christ Jesus.
In his Word is our hope.
    If we confess our sins, he is faithful and just to forgive us our sins and
        to cleanse us from all unrighteousness.
"Faithful and just"—divine attributes that are alien to our nature.
You are reliable,
    consistent,
    dependable,
        utterly true to your holy nature.
With you, God, there is absolutely no duplicity,
    only absolute dependability.
That is why we rely on the promise of your Word—
    that with our confession of sins committed
    and belief in the cleansing of our hearts by faith,
    we have the charge of "unrighteousness" removed from our record
    and the righteousness of Christ imputed to us.
Desiring such a divine transaction, we now confess our sins to you.

{ SILENT PRAYER }

Thanks and praise be to God, for he has promised the removal of all
    unrighteousness.

Calvary's detergent makes us clean—
  now, no condemnation;
    now, peace with God.
This is good news:
  We who are cleansed are reconciled.
May we be more thankful for your daily mercies.
May we be humble under your correction.
May we be zealous in doing your will.
May we be watchful against temptation.
May we be content under trial.
May we be what we profess.

Great Shepherd of the sheep—
Look with compassion upon our number experiencing the valley
    of shadows,
  unpleasant, painful, disconcerting—
    yea, devastating troubles affect some here today.
May the presence of Jesus penetrate such awful gloom and give joyful
    victory to all who feel abandoned.
May all leave this place rejoicing and saying,
  "It was good to be in God's house today."

                                                              ✝ Amen.

---

1 John 1:9; 1 Corinthians 6:11, NLT

Children's Day Prayer

Blessed are you, O God,
Father of our Lord Jesus Christ.
By your abundant mercy we have been born anew—
    to a living hope, through the resurrection of Jesus Christ from the dead,
    to an inheritance which is imperishable, undefiled and unfading,
    kept in heaven for us.
Such anticipation evokes a heart of continued thanksgiving.
    May our praise to you arise, as it were, as *sweet smelling incense.*
On this Children's Sunday, those of us who had loving parents
    who worshiped God,
        considered their *children a gift from God,* and
        endeavored to teach us, very early, the way of salvation
            are privileged, Lord.
So today we thank you, Father God, for
    our parents,
    our teachers,
    our pastors,
    our mentors,
who have loved us, taught us, prayed with us and for us,
    and lived before us as *men and women of faith.*

We thank you, God, for the many teachers and volunteers in this church,
    who give biblical instruction each week.
We ask, Lord Jesus, that each one entrusted to our care would come
    to know you as

Savior,
Redeemer,
Protector,
the Guardian along life's pathways.

We pray for all those children in this church who have been dedicated
  to the Lord over the years.
We have covenanted to pray for them. We do so now.
  Fulfill in each one the prayers for them on that sacred occasion.

Blessed Jesus, we have much to learn in the school of prayer:
  We begin with the words you taught the disciples to pray, praying:
Our Father which art in heaven,
hallowed be thy name.
Thy kingdom come,
thy will be done in earth,
  as it is in heaven.
Give us this day our daily bread.
And forgive us our debts,
  as we forgive our debtors.
And lead us not into temptation,
  but deliver us from evil.
For thine is the kingdom, and the power, and the glory, for ever.

✢ *Amen.*

---

1 Peter 1:3-4; Psalm 141:2; Psalm 127:3, NLT; Galatians 3:9; Matthew 6:9-13, KJV

MAY

Let us cast ourselves down before the majesty of our good God,
conscious of our faults, praying that He may not only forgive us,
but may daily cleanse us of them.

JOHN CALVIN

Everlasting God, Lover of our souls,
Open our eyes to see your love for us—
  your love which was established before creation
  and continues unfailing and unending, even unto this very hour.
Your Word tells us that *you had a plan for us a long, long time ago.*
A love for us not based on
  performance,
  or beauty,
  or inherent value.
A love which sent a Savior to the unlovely,
  the destitute,
  the helpless,
  the condemned.
A Savior whose love prompted him to say:
  "Come unto me all you who are heavy laden, and I will give you rest."

Lord, may you this day be the *present help* of all who turn to you,
  whether hurt or ashamed,
  whether sick or disheartened,
  whether afraid or defeated,
  whether troubled or angry.
You have come to change the human condition drastically, totally . . .
  the sinful heart,
  the stony heart,
  the rebellious heart.

Holy physician, divine surgeon . . . work in our lives that our souls might
  prosper in spiritual health and vitality.
Do this in the life of every person now praying to you.

{ SILENT PRAYER }

Thank you, Lord,
  for hearing,
  for answering,
  for meeting every need.

✢ Amen.

Ephesians 1:4, NLT; Matthew 11:28; Psalm 46:1

Mother's Day Prayer

Blessed God of all grace, God of salvation,
God of comfort and the essence of a thousand other descriptions—
we cannot adequately nor fully describe you.
From hearts softened and awakened to the gospel,
liberated from the penalty of sin,
cleansed from the stain of sin,
indwelt by the Holy Guest,
prepared for an eternal dwelling in a city
whose builder and maker is God—
We praise you that mere man when *born again* can then love you and enjoy
you forever.
This is all your doing,
your initiative,
your completion—
yours alone.
To God be the glory,
Great things he has done.
It was not my interest before, but now
help me to *seek first your kingdom and your righteousness.*
You know what I need *even before I ask.*
May I never think I prosper unless my soul prospers—
or that I am rich unless rich toward you,
or that I am wise unless *wise unto salvation.*
May I value all things in relation to eternity.

Many of us in this place today praise you for the blessed memory
   of a Christian home.
Our prayers of thanksgiving join those of Timothy,
   for the incredible blessing of learning the Holy Scriptures at a *mother's*
      and a grandmother's knee.
We thank you, Father God, for our mothers who have loved us—
   taught us—
   prayed with us and for us—
   and lived before us as women of faith.
   May that heritage continue on in this generation.

Prepare our hearts to receive the seed of your Word.
   Grant that it may take deep root and bring forth fruit to your glory.
   Visit us with your salvation and instill faith in every heart.

✝ **A**men.

John 3:3; Fanny Crosby, "To God Be the Glory"; Matthew 6:33; Matthew 6:8;
2 Timothy 3:15, KJV; 2 Timothy 1:5; Psalm 106:4

Blessed be the God and Father of our Lord Jesus Christ,
The *Father of all mercies and the God of all comfort.*
We praise you that we are not left to despair,
    For your mercy is more than sufficient and plenteous in application.
    Your comfort, so necessary in present circumstances, is a balm to my soul.

Lord Jesus Christ, we are sorry for the things we have done wrong in the
    living of these days.
    We look within and are repulsed by the meanness, and ugliness, and
        weakness of our lives.
We now turn from everything that we know is wrong,
    from moodiness and irritability,
    from insensitivity and carelessness of the feelings of others.
We seek your forgiveness.

{ SILENT PRAYER }

Thank you, mighty Savior, that you willingly died on the cross for us,
    so that we could be forgiven and set free.
Thank you, wonderful Savior, that you offer forgiveness and the gift of your
    Spirit: I now receive that gift.
I ask you, Lord,
    rule my heart,
    my passions,
    my thoughts,
    my words.

So strengthen us by the Holy Spirit that in the days to come we may lead
lives more pleasing to you.
Make our hearts your temple in which you supremely dwell—possessing
us with such indestructible joy that day by day
we are conformed more and more to Christ's glad image.

Father God, remember those who are suffering in the world—
the orphans, the victims of earthquakes, floods, and disease.
May helping hands be not denied.
We rejoice with all those who count their blessings and we praise you with
all those today who hear the gospel invitation and respond,
"Lord, I believe."

✛ *Amen.*

---

2 Corinthians 1:3; Romans 8:29; John 11:27

Pentecost Prayer

God who promises us the Holy Comforter,
We praise your holy name for your marvelous loving-kindness and your
 many gifts.
Especially this Pentecost Sunday, we give you thanks for the promised
 outpouring of the Holy Spirit.
Jesus said:
 *"I will not leave you as orphans; the Father will give you the Holy Spirit who
 will never leave you and will lead you into all truth."*
And so we praise you, Father God,
 for all the gifts and graces of the Holy Spirit bestowed on believers
 and manifested in the lives of those who walk by faith.

We thank you for *love, joy, peace, longsuffering, gentleness, goodness, faith,
 meekness, temperance*—
 may such fruit be abounding in this congregation.
We praise you for all who through the Holy Spirit have been convinced
 of sin and led to repentance.
We praise you for all who by the Holy Spirit's indwelling are enabled
 to live a holier, more Christlike life.
Continue your gracious work in our lives.
 Indwell us as Power—
 expelling every desire to sin, enabling us to live victoriously.
 Indwell us as Sanctifier—
 reigning supreme in every aspect of our lives.

Indwell us as Teacher—
    leading us to a better understanding of our salvation.
Indwell us as Paraclete—
    that we may never grieve you nor resist you.

Grant that through the Holy Spirit we may be enabled
    to live and walk in this world as those who are no longer in bondage
        to sin—
    but set at liberty in Christ, with our eyes set on our eternal home.
Praise the ever-living God who meets the needs of his people.

                          ✣ *Amen.*

John 14:16-18, NLT; Galatians 5:22-23, KJV

Memorial Day Prayer

Gracious God, eternal Father,
Who has created us in your image and whose glory was revealed
    in the face of Jesus Christ,
    grant us to know Christ and his life,
        that the *same mind which was in him may be in us.*
By your abundant mercy,
    we have been born anew to a living hope
    through the resurrection of Jesus Christ from the dead,
    to an inheritance which is imperishable, undefiled, and unfading,
    kept in heaven for us
    where neither rust can corrupt nor thieves break in and steal.
We praise you for such redemption.
You rescued us from the *broad road that leads to destruction—*
    and turned our hearts toward the narrow path that leads
        heavenward.
Though heaven is our home, we don't always manifest a heavenly
        spirit.
For such failures in speech, attitudes, and actions,
    we fervently ask for your forgiveness.

{ SILENT PRAYER }

Thank you, Father, for forgiveness—full and free.
Now may we heed the Lord's words:
    "Go and sin no more."

Lord Jesus, there are many needs represented in this congregation—
 needs greater than our ability to alleviate,
  but they are no challenge to you.
This day, may you provide, out of your abundance, sustaining grace
  to the grieving,
 the lonely,
 the financially burdened,
 the unemployed,
 those who suffer broken relationships,
 those in troubling circumstances,
  those facing secret battles against almost overwhelming temptations.
Many face debilitating health issues.
 Lord, have mercy and grant a healing touch to them.

Father God, we thank you for those of yesteryear who left home and family
  to defend our country;
 we enjoy the fruit of their sacrifice—we worship you in freedom.
Remember your children worldwide who want to worship you openly,
  but dare not.
 Grant openness to the gospel in those places of satanic oppression.
 Remember those of our extended family required to be in harm's way
  and all our military family.
 Keep them from hurt and destruction.
 Shield them from all harm.
 Enable them to boldly and faithfully live a Christian life,
  and may their testimony before fellow soldiers bear eternal fruit.
We pray all conflicts will end speedily
 and the gospel's power will permeate all those troubled lands.
Give divine wisdom to our national leaders
 that they may govern in ways that honor you.

✝ *Amen.*

---

1 Corinthians 2:16; 1 Peter 1:3-4; Matthew 7:13; John 8:11

JUNE

What the *Book of Common Prayer* says about marriage can readily be applied to public prayer as well. It "is not to be entered into lightly or carelessly, but reverently and in the fear of God."

WARREN WIERSBE

Blessed Redeemer, beautiful Savior,
Author of all grace and comfort.
We approach you with the deepest reverence—
  not with any presumption, nor with servile fear—
  but with respectful boldness—because of your gracious invitation.
In days of yore, you met the invited penitent at the *mercy seat.*
  There the sprinkled blood was a covering for sin.
Today, our needed blessings are to be found at the *throne of grace.*
  Here it is that *we find grace in every—every—every! time of need.*

It is easy for us to elaborate our needs, as trouble upon trouble piles up on us:
  fragmented friendships,
  hostile relationships,
  adversarial conditions,
  financial roadblocks,
  family nightmares,
  unanswered questions.
Some of these heartburning situations have plagued us without relief,
  and we have pled with you to alleviate—
    yet still we wait for a divine answer.
Lord, we have nowhere else to go but to you,
  and so we again cast ourselves upon your mercy.
Maybe you delay because of the insidious sins
  we tolerate or turn a blind eye to!

Galatians tells of good old Barnabas and influential Simon Peter who were
   captured by flagrant hypocrisy.
Maybe that's our sin today—protection of self—
   desiring the approval of the crowd rather than God.
Father God, it will take a detergent as strong as the blood of Jesus Christ
   to wash away that sin.
We confess with tears all the times we played the hypocrite
   and curried the world's favor—in the world's place—
   and tried some face-saving, self-serving falseness around God's people.
Forgive us, Lord, as we pray now for deliverance from such sin.

{ SILENT PRAYER }

Thank you, Father; help us to never again indulge in hypocrisy.
In the name of Jesus, *the way, the truth, and the life.*

✝ *Amen.*

Leviticus 16:14; Hebrews 4:16; Galatians 2:11-13; John 14:6

Father God, author and finisher of our faith,
Source of every blessing we enjoy,
  how great are our privileges in Christ Jesus.
Bountiful is your provision for all our needs—
  our sin is that we do not appropriate what is available.
You are *able to keep us from stumbling*.
But as we review even this past week, we've stumbled so many times:
  stumbled in relationships,
  stumbled with wrong attitudes,
  stumbled in temptation.
Forgive me for stumbling when I need not have.
Keep me from stumbling:
  be my arm of support,
  my strength,
  my stability.

You have promised to *present me blameless.*
When I consider my faults—and think of being presented in glory, faultless—
  I am overcome with gratitude to you, my Savior,
  my Paraclete, my **advocate**—thank you, thank you.
You have said you will present me **with great joy**.
Oh Lord, help us to finish the race set before each one of us—
  to persevere,
  to walk in faith,
  to love you supremely,

and like Abraham, to have an eye on *that city*
  which has foundations, whose builder and maker is God,
that we might be presented with great joy.
Heaven rejoiced on the day of our repentance, and now you promise
  rejoicing on our presentation!
All this is promised because you alone are our Savior—
  we absolutely do not rely on anything or anyone but you.
So fulfill this promise to us today:
  Unto him that is able to keep you from stumbling,
  and to present you faultless before the presence of his glory, with exceeding joy,
  to the only God, our Savior, be glory and majesty, dominion and power,
  both now and ever.

✣ 𝔄men.

Jude 1:24; Colossians 1:22; Hebrews 11:10; Jude 1:24-25

Eternal God, everlasting Father,
Great and marvelous are your works.
When we really contemplate you as Creator and sustainer of all things,
   we are overawed by your greatness.
The flowers of the field are of greater beauty than Solomon in all his glory.
The *sparrow is the recipient of your provision,*
   the object of your watch and care.
Nations and rulers are in place at your will and by your decree.
Events totally beyond our control
   are subject to your purpose and determined will.
And in between sparrows and nations,
   you extend your providential care to your children.

You, O God, asked Abraham: *"Is anything too hard for the Lord?"*
We need to have such truth reinforced in our thinking—
   for the enemy of our souls besieges us with doubts
      about your involvement in our lives.
We are overwhelmed with contrary circumstances,
   and we are sometimes almost drowning in despair.
We confess that we have almost made security and money our idols,
      thinking that investments and governments would see us through.
   Now we need to realize there is absolutely no security except in you.
You, Father God, are our secure provision.

We need to pray and praise like Mary,
   The Lord took notice of his servant and has done great things for me.

May that be our testimony this day.
Individually, we now confess our sins, plead forgiveness, and trust you
    for daily bread.

{ SILENT PRAYER }

Thank you, Father, for a cleansed heart and a renewed spirit.
Thank you for meeting every need.

✝ Amen.

Luke 12:27; Luke 12:7; Genesis 18:14; Luke 1:48-49, NLT

Blessed be the name of the Lord.
In expressing our praise to you, Mighty God, we can do no more than
    echo David's words when he prayed:
    Yours, O Lord, is the greatness and the power
    and the glory and the victory and the majesty,
    indeed everything that is in the heavens and the earth;
    Yours is the dominion, O Lord, and you exalt yourself as head over all.
    Both riches and honor come from you, and you rule over all,
    and in your hand is power and might;
    and it lies in your hand to make great
    and to strengthen every one.
    Now therefore, our God, we thank you, and praise your glorious name.

Holy Father, we believe your Word to be absolutely true—that you rule
    over everything—
    not a single molecule in the universe exists apart from your
        superintendence.
So nothing can touch us,
    harm us,
    ruin us,
and ultimately your eternal purposes will be fulfilled.
Praise your everlasting name.

We bless you, Lord, and endeavor to *never forget the good things you do* for us.
As the psalmist says:

You forgive all my sins,
heal all my diseases,
ransom me from death—
and surround me with love and tender mercies.
You fill my life with good things.
That is my testimony.
Whether in the dark valley,
　or through troubled waters,
　or surrounded by enemy forces,
　　you prepare a table before me—you provide for me.
I am restored!
I praise your name—today, tomorrow, and forever.

✝ Amen.

1 Chronicles 29:11-13, NASB; Psalm 103:2, 3-5, NLT; Psalm 23:5

JULY

In all my prayers for you, I always pray with joy, being confident of this,
that he who began a good work in you will carry it on
to completion until the day of Christ Jesus.

THE APOSTLE PAUL

Independence Day Prayer

Divine ruler of men and of nations,
We thank you for those of yesteryear who came to these shores to lay the
foundation of civil and religious liberty.
We are grateful for everyone who in perilous times took up the sword and
paid the ultimate sacrifice, that we might live in peace and freedom.
As great as that blessing is, it pales in comparison to being set free
from the burden of sin—
enabled to live in righteousness
and worship God with hearts made clean
through the sacrifice of Jesus Christ, our Savior.

Today, we pray for those who lead our nation,
that they might be granted wisdom to lead in
honesty,
integrity,
fairness—
For *righteousness exalts a nation, but sin is a disgrace to any people.*
In these days of immense national and international turmoil,
we pray you will give to those in all levels of government
a desire to promote justice and live in truth.
O gracious Lord God, you *have called us out of darkness into your
marvelous light.*
We bless you because you are *the Rock of our salvation.*
You are solid and sure and steadfast.
Grant that the gospel might be heard in all corners of the earth.

We pray for gathered believers around the world—
  The bride of Christ—awaiting *the marriage supper of the Lamb.*
We pray for our local church, that it might be a sign here on earth of the
    church that shall be gathered above.
Grant that this congregation
  may be firmly established in Christ,
  built up in Christ,
  performing the work of Christ,
  filled with the love of Christ.
We pray for the members of your body:
  for husbands and wives—
    that their love for each other might be ever richer and kinder;
  for children and young people—
    that they may grow in their trust of you and experience your gracious
      leadership in the decisions of life;
  for people who live alone—
    that they might find community here and a deepening companionship
      with you;
  for the elderly—
    that they might reflect the godly radiance which belongs to those whose
      walk with you demonstrates spiritual maturity;
  for those who serve in the military—
    that they might be protected from destruction and live exemplary lives;
  for the ill and afflicted—
    that the presence of Christ will be ever more real in their lives.
All these mercies we ask in the name of Jesus who is our intercessor.

✝ *Amen.*

Proverbs 14:34, NIV; 1 Peter 2:9; Psalm 95:1; Revelation 19:9; Ephesians 3:17-19

Independence Day Prayer

Gracious God, Father of real freedom,
Deliverer from bondage to all who seek your face,
We pray the prayer of David in the Psalms, who pleaded,
   "Bring my soul out of prison."
Yes, Lord,
free us from the penitentiary of our sins,
   free us from the handcuffs of guilt—
   we are captured and restrained by the deception
      that our way is better than yours.
Free us from the prison of hopelessness—
   thinking that our situation is beyond help or change.
Free us from the high walls of our fears—
   fears of today and fears of tomorrow.
Free us from the confines of our foolish rebellion to your laws and
      your Word.
Unlock the door that keeps us in our cell of selfish living—
   callous actions,
   thankless murmurings,
   and unjustified complaints.
Free us from the leg irons of hypocrisy—
   those deceptions that make us think our duplicity fools you.
Free us from the jailhouse of unbelief.
Deliverance is our need—deliverance from the captivity of sins!

"Bring my soul out of prison, that I may praise your name."
That is our gracious privilege today—
    to praise you for complete deliverance
        from the guilt,
        from the power,
        from the judgment of sin.
Keep us in the freedom of experiencing your salvation—constantly,
    free to enjoy you—now, today, and forever.

Lord Jesus, we plead for your magnified grace to be upon those of our number
    who face—in various forms—the enemy of health and vitality.
    Give grace and strength to caregivers.
    Comfort the grieving.
    Fulfill your promises to those who believe.
This we earnestly pray, in the strong name of Jesus, our Savior.

        ✦ Amen.

Psalm 142:7

Blessed and glorious God,
Author of our salvation, sustainer of our life, giver of all that we have—
   incline our hearts to believe your Word.
We are so obsessed with trivial things, but we want to be captivated with
      things eternal.
So much of little worth gets our attention.
   We confess inattention to your Word.
   We confess the fickleness of our affections,
      and our unbelief limits our trust that you, O God, are
able to do exceedingly abundantly above all that we can ask or think.

We don't see our prayers answered with such abundance, and so we doubt.
We know our problems are greater than we can solve.
But we are afraid to go out on a limb and really cast our care on you.
   What if you don't answer as we want?
   What if a much-needed job doesn't appear?
   What if family relationships don't improve—but get worse?
   What if loved ones remain disinterested in spiritual things?
   What if my desperate heart's cry goes unanswered?

Lord, I'm not like Habakkuk,
   who witnessed everything crashing around him
      and still *rejoiced in the Lord.*

I confess that I'm *like Asaph,*
   who realized how bitter he had become
      at the bewildering events of life.

But, like the psalmist, we've come to the *house of the Lord* this morning.
It is here that we see things more clearly.
You will guide me,
  counsel me,
  strengthen my resolve,
  shelter me in the storms,
  steady my footsteps,
  meet my needs,
  quiet my soul.
My prayer from the depths of my heart is joined with those here:
  Deliver us from foolish charges, senseless complaints, ignorant doubts.
  Saturate our souls with the greatness of Christ!
  Make our faith in Christ and his goodness unshakable.
  Make our trust in Christ so absolute that nothing can erode it.
    We believe; *help thou our unbelief.*
May we not stagger at the promises of God.

So we pray the words you taught the disciples to pray:
Our Father which art in heaven,
hallowed be thy name.
Thy kingdom come,
thy will be done in earth,
  as it is in heaven.
Give us this day our daily bread.
And forgive us our debts,
  as we forgive our debtors.
And lead us not into temptation,
  but deliver us from evil.
For thine is the kingdom, and the power, and the glory, for ever.

                                        ✝ *Amen.*

Ephesians 3:20; Habakkuk 3:18; Psalm 73:21; Psalm 122:1; Mark 9:24; Matthew 6:9-13, KJV

God of compassion,
God who is *rich in mercy* to all those who call upon you,
   we come to you, humbly confessing our sins.
We confess
   our sinful affections on misplaced values,
   the prideful arrogance of our willfulness,
   the attachments we nurse to self-justification,
   the brazen questioning of your goodness and love,
   the doubts we harbor about the reliability of your promises.
These sins, and many more, we now confess.
Believing that you, Lord, are
   faithful and just to forgive us and cleanse us from all unrighteousness.
Hear, Father, our confessions.

{ SILENT PRAYER }

Now, by your grace and strength, may we, like the forgiven sinner
   of Jesus' day,
   Go out and sin no more.

Father God, this past week we have been emotionally pulled by
   circumstances and events that left us in disarray.
   We needed divine assurance that your grace would be sufficient to see
     us through.
And now in this place of worship,

we believe God's *grace is sufficient*—
   and that this sufficiency is without limit.
Grace sufficient to hold me,
   sufficient to strengthen me,
   sufficient to shield me from eternal harm,
   sufficient to help me triumph over every difficulty,
   sufficient to provide for me all the way to heaven.
No longer am I afraid,
   no longer defeated,
   for I believe at this very moment—and for every day remaining—
      that the grace of the Lord Jesus Christ is sufficient.
All these mercies we ask in the name of Jesus, who is our intercessor.

✦ *Amen.*

Ephesians 2:4; 1 John 1:9; John 8:11; 2 Corinthians 12:9

AUGUST

May our Master be with us, and by his grace
reveal our Lord Jesus Christ . . . so that by the eyes of faith
every one of you . . . may now be enabled to look unto him
who was crucified for our sins, who bore our griefs,
and carried away our sorrows.

C. H. SPURGEON

God whose power is limitless,
King of kings and Lord of lords, to whom all authority belongs,
   whose sovereignty embraces all creation.
We praise you that you are our *Alpha and Omega,*
   our beginning and our end.
      Apart from you there is nothing.
You, blessed Spirit of God, have given us eyes to see our sin and our need
   of a Savior.
You have brought us to saving faith in the *Lamb of God,* who takes away
   sin and gives eternal life.
We now confess our sins . . . repent of our sins . . . and by your grace and
   power, turn from them.
Hear, O Lord, our confessions . . . our prayers.

{ SILENT PRAYER }

We walk in newness of life—but not on "easy" street.
   Some of us struggle on *a hill called Difficulty* . . .
   Others wander in *By-Path Meadow* . . .
   Some are trapped in *the Slough of Despond* . . .
   A few are held captive by *Giant Despair in Doubting Castle* . . .
      and then there are those charmed by *Vanity Fair* . . .
Give us a renewed vision of the *Delectable Mountains.*
Bring us . . . each one of us . . . to the *narrow way,*
   the straight way,

the more excellent way,
the new and living way—
   the Jesus way.

We believe that if we walk in truth, we walk with you,
and like the *Emmaus travelers*, we'll have a joyous experience—
   turning our sadness into satisfaction.
It is in the name of Jesus
   we pray and believe.

                                                    ✢ Amen.

---

1 Timothy 6:15; Daniel 7:14; Revelation 22:13; John 1:29; John Bunyan, *Pilgrim's Progress*;
Matthew 7:13-14; Luke 24:13-34

Most glorious God, God of compassion, God of forgiveness,
I need your presence.
Great Physician, I need healing.
   I am spiritually lukewarm
   and unbelief mars my confidence in trusting you—
      brokenness and repeated failures occupy my attention.
It astounds me that I continually try to battle life's issues on my own.
   Sin makes me forget you.
Too long I have neglected the closet of prayer . . .
Too long I have forsaken the refreshment of your Word . . .
The cobwebs of indifference and the dust of life's cares choke my soul.
Broken relationships and shattered trust have prevented the health and
      healing of your Word.

But now—this moment,
I turn from absenteeism to the *mercy seat*.
   I praise you for permission to approach the *throne of grace*.
Here, I pour out my confession of sin:
   neglect,
   pride,
   willfulness,
   arrogance,
   self-sufficiency,
      foolishly questioning your providence.
Divinely sweep away my soul's clutter.

Pour down upon me streams of needful grace.
Engage my heart to live more faithfully for you.
Your presence alone can make me holy,
devout,
strong,
happy.
I praise you for forgiveness—
real,
comprehensive,
enabling.
Accomplish in me your eternal purposes, through Jesus Christ,
my only hope, my only Savior.

✢ Amen.

Matthew 9:12; Exodus 25:22; Hebrews 4:16

Holy Father, God of our salvation,
We take refuge in your divinely appointed sanctuary—
    the covert, the asylum—
    where we are protected from the condemnation and judgment of sin.
Once upon a time we did not care about our sinful condition.
    Sin was fun, righteousness was old-fashioned.
        God? Unnecessary.
        Salvation? Irrelevant.
But everlasting thanks to you, glorious God,
    friend of sinners,
    rescuer of the perishing—
You tenderized my heart,
    opened my eyes,
    enlightened my understanding,
    sanitized my desires,
        directed my pathway.
And now *the God of peace,*
    the great Shepherd,
    through the blood of the everlasting covenant, works in me to do his will.
O let us praise God!
    May the praise of your people never cease.

We gladly give thanks for your goodness, which is our daily benefit.
    Your provisions for us surprise us continually.
    Your mercies refresh us in every time of need.

Praise be to God, we are never placed on some "quota" system—
   you have never said to any of your beloved,
"That's all the grace you get, lest I run out."
   No, never . . . never!
We are promised *grace for every time of need.*
I shall list all my needs—every one—and still your grace is sufficient.
   Economic quandaries?
   Health issues?
   Difficult decisions?
   Troublesome relationships?
   Sinful allurements?
   Failed plans and promises?
   Unanswered prayers?
These, and more, we leave with you, assured that as our Great Shepherd,
   you will care for your sheep.
Evermore do we rest in you, O Lord, *our strength and our Redeemer.*

✝ Amen.

Hebrews 13:20; Philippians 2:13; Hebrews 4:16; John 10:1-18; Psalm 19:14

Almighty God, King over all,
Majesty and strength are your characteristics.
Your reign is firmly established, from everlasting to everlasting.
Generations preceding us have seen your Word fulfilled,
    and generations to come will find your Word absolutely reliable.
As Zechariah the prophet has said:
"The Lord Almighty has done what he said he would do."
You have promised a Savior . . .
    and the Savior has come.
You have promised a "once for all" atonement for sin . . .
    and that atonement has been made.
You have promised reconciliation with sinners . . .
    and we have experienced forgiveness.
You have promised the Paraclete . . .
    and the Comforter has come.

We praise you for your goodness,
    which is displayed to us daily.
We praise you for your keeping power,
    which has preserved us in all our circumstances.
We praise you for your mercies,
    which have strengthened us times without number.
We praise you that you will never declare null and void your divinely
        established promises to your people.

So now we confess our sin of
  ignoring your Word,
  doubting your Word,
  resisting your Word.
    Hear now our confessions.

{ SILENT PRAYER }

Thank you, Father God, for forgiveness, reconciliation, fellowship.
Prepare our hearts to receive the seed of your Word as it is preached.
Grant that it may take deep root and bring forth fruit to your glory.
  Arouse the careless among us,
  humble the self-righteous,
  soften the hardened,
  encourage the fearful,
  deliver the doubting,
  comfort the grieving,
    bring many to repentance, belief, and salvation.
And in all of us grant a willingness to readily and gladly obey your Word.

✝ Amen.

Psalm 93:2; Zechariah 1:6

Great Shepherd of the sheep,
We take comfort in the fact that you are the God of providence.
Your ways are far beyond us.
We wrestle to make sense of the difficulties we face.
Sometimes our trust in you wavers as we try to believe
  that what you allow to happen to us is for our own good.
We struggle with today while you are directing us toward tomorrow.
  Help us to really trust you.

We think of Joseph, obediently taking Mary and the young child Jesus
  and *fleeing to Egypt.*
  Refugees they were, in a strange land, among a strange culture.
Were they befriended?
Did people of faith house them, feed them, help Joseph find work?
Others of Holy Scripture were also refugees:
  Moses, David,
  Priscilla and Aquila,
    and hundreds of post-Pentecost believers living in Jerusalem.
Today the world is spotted with millions of refugees.
Lord God, bless the efforts of all those who are engaged in the tasks
  of alleviating the human suffering of refugees,
    particularly those who minister in the name of Jesus.

Our attention is drawn to the many refugees in our neighborhoods.
Some are neighbors living in isolation,
  struggling to exist, desperate in their condition.

Make us, Lord, kind in thought,
   gentle in word,
   generous in deed
      to the *alien in our midst*.
Perhaps, Lord, you have brought these people from distant lands
      to this place
   that they might be shown the love of Jesus
      and come to know the gospel's truth.
Lord, don't let us fail you.
Teach us that *it is better to give than to receive*—
   better to minister than to be ministered to.
Anoint us with godliness that we might *love our neighbor as ourselves*.

We pray today that the preaching of your Word will not fall upon deaf ears.
Convict the sinner and remove the sin,
   counsel the confused and lead the way,
   comfort the grieving and give peace, sweet peace,
      refresh those *thirsting for righteousness*.
Answer to your glory we pray, in Jesus' name.

✝ *Amen.*

Isaiah 55:8, NLT; Matthew 2:13; Leviticus 19:34, NIV; Acts 20:35;
Mark 12:31; Matthew 5:6

SEPTEMBER

As a pastor I am impressed that leading a congregation in prayer
to God is a significant and responsible act. I am well aware that God
is gracious and hears us, not because we say it well, but because we come
in faith through the Lord Jesus Christ.

ROBERT N. SCHAPER

Living, holy, eternal God,
We come to you trusting not in any work of our hands but in your matchless
   invitation,
   "Come unto me, all you who labor and are heavy laden,
   and I will give you rest."
   Rest—from self-imposed activity attempting to impress you, God.
   Rest—from self-loathing due to dominating sin.
   Rest—from the pressures and failures of self-directed living.
   Rest—from the fear of God's departure.
We take refuge in the name of Jesus . . . . *Immanuel . . . God with us.*
Praise the Lord; you have not departed from us.
   You do not pay us transient visits.
      You are with us forever.
We rejoice in this good news—
   we are enabled,
   we are safe,
   we are at peace.
God's bank account is more than sufficient to meet our every situation,
   for *he is able to do exceedingly abundantly,*
      surpassing above all that we can ask or think.
God is with us.

Faithful God, wonderful Savior, we boldly bring to you the promise you
   make to us:
   The desire of the righteous shall be granted.

Father, our greatest, never-lessening desire is for the salvation of our
   loved ones.
Across our assembled congregation, communities, and neighborhoods
   are burdened hearts . . .
   for children, brothers, sisters, extended family—
   dear ones living apart from God,
   living in unbelief,
   living under judgment . . .
   and bound for a Christless eternity.
Lord, you are a *seeking shepherd* as well as a saving shepherd.
You sought us who believe, and we have hope for those laid upon our
   hearts in prayer:
   Seek them out too.

We pray for our descendants throughout all generations.
   We know that which is born of the flesh is flesh and nothing more.
Lord, make them to *be born anew*
   under your covenant of grace by your Holy Spirit.
   Be their Savior even as you are mine.
We have prayed this, times without number, but your Word encourages
   us to pray again.
   We pray boldly, unselfishly, earnestly, urgently, believingly.
We pray in Jesus' name—right now by name—for our unsaved relatives.

{ SILENT PRAYER }

And now, like Habakkuk, we shall *go to our tower and watch the Lord answer
   prayer!*

✢ 𝔄men.

Matthew 11:28; Matthew 1:23; Ephesians 3:20; Proverbs 10:24; Matthew 18:12-14;
John 3:6; Habakkuk 2:1

Holy God, Lord most gracious,
We are in great need and you have extended your beneficent invitation:
  "Come unto me, all you who are heavy laden."
That describes us: we are overloaded with the cares of our existence.
We are creatures of need, but there is a problem . . .
What we see as our need is not the way you see it.
  We see our need as more money;
  we see our need as better health;
  we see our need as a promotion;
  as greater respect from our family;
    as less anxiety—less stress—less pressure.
You see our need as prioritizing:
  Seek first the kingdom of God and his righteousness.
We confess that really, deep down, we don't love you with all our hearts.
  Lord, we see our sin. Forgive us.
In these moments of worship, we want to love you first and foremost.
  Help us to experience the joy of love unblemished, a life lived to please God.
We pray that we will know you, whom to know is life more abundant.
We want to join with the psalmist in saying,
  As the deer longs for streams of water,
    So I long for you, O God.
  I thirst for God, the living God.

✟ 𝔄men.

Matthew 11:28; Matthew 6:33; Psalm 42:1-2, NLT

Eternal God, and our Father,
You have brought us to this day and to this place.
We haven't always recognized your involvement in our lives.
    Indeed, we shunned the very idea of sin
        and guilt and judgment to come.
We scorned the idea of atonement and the necessity of right standing
    before a holy God.

We were *dead in our iniquities,*
    having no eyes to see you,
    no ears to hear you,
    no intelligence to know you.
We were not merely bystanders to the cosmic conflict—
    we were **enemies**, in rebellion to the King of Glory.
Indifferent to the ways of grace and ignorant of our destitute condition,
    we did not comprehend or care
        that the gulf between us and you was so great
        there was no possibility of reconciliation.

But praise be to God, you alone are
    the initiator,
    the seeker,
    the reconciler,
    the wooer of my soul.
Drawn by cords of divine love,
    you gave me faith to believe, to trust, to obey.

Delivered from the kingdom of darkness and death, and standing *blameless before you,*
   I can now join the blood-bought throng and sing:
      Oh, the love that drew salvation's plan!
      Oh, the grace that brought it down to man!
      Oh, the mighty gulf that God did span . . . at Calvary!
You have *begun a good work in me and you will complete it.*

Grant me never to lose sight of
   the exceeding sinfulness of sin,
   the exceeding righteousness of salvation,
   the exceeding glory of Christ,
      the exceeding wonder of grace.
When my heart listens to doubts . . . and grows cold in love toward you . . .
   forgive such terrible sin and *refresh my memory in the joys of salvation.*
We thank you now for *your mercies, fresh every morning.*

✢ *Amen.*

Ephesians 2:1; Ephesians 2:8; Ephesians 5:27, NIV; William Newell, "At Calvary";
Philippians 1:6; Psalm 51:12; Lamentations 3:23

Majestic God, who extends mercy,
We acknowledge your Son, the Lord Jesus Christ,
  as our only Savior, the Preeminent One.
He is the Creator of the earth
  and all that lies therein.
He is the governor of the universe,
  Judge of the living and the dead,
  Head of the church,
    Savior of sinners.

Sovereign Lord, your *greatness is unsearchable.*
  Your goodness is infinite.
  Your compassion unfailing.
    Your mercies, ever new.
You are altogether lovely—superior in all things.
You are our only refuge,
  our only foundation,
  our *only hope,*
    our only confidence.

Grant us, in our brokenness and fear,
  to gather courage from the fact that *you hold all things together.*
Open our eyes to see the fullness of your excellence.
Remove the lopsided and distorted images of Jesus
  that weaken our worship

and hinder our obedience
and prevent our growth.
We try to shoehorn our desires and wishes into circumstances and attitudes
that are ill-fitting to those who claim your sovereignty.
We are afraid to let go of that which we mistakenly think we control for fear
everything will fall apart—
when in reality, you, the supreme One, hold all things together.
Help us to grow in the knowledge and conviction of your preeminence,
letting you take reign—
in our home,
in our business,
in our plans,
in all our relationships.
We pray, O Lord, *that as we confess our sins,*
your wonderful forgiveness will wash over us,
cleansing from all unrighteousness.

{ SILENT PRAYER }

Thank you, Lord Jesus.

✢ Amen.

Acts 10:42; Colossians 1:18; Job 5:9; Lamentations 3:22-23; Psalm 71:5, NIV;
Colossians 1:17, NIV; 1 John 1:9

Almighty God, sovereign Creator, gracious Redeemer,
We *call you Father* because, by your grace, you have
   called us,
   drawn us,
   welcomed us,
   forgiven us,
   removed from us our *status as enemies*—
      and made us to be *new creatures in Christ Jesus.*
Now we have eyes to see and hearts to obey your gracious words.

Believing that **you alone** *do all things well*, we can pray with Job,
   "The Lord gives and the Lord takes away—
     blessed be the name of the Lord."
Or with Hannah,
   "The Lord makes poor and makes rich;
     the Lord brings low or exalts."
We believe it is your hand that gives or withholds.

Many around us cannot trust the wisdom, power, and goodness of Christ
   in the midst of inexplicable suffering
   or calamity
   or loss
     or baffling circumstances.
So when we are puzzled by events that test our trust,
we earnestly pray that you will incline our hearts to your Word

and to its assurances that you will work
all things according to the counsel of your will,
that no purpose of yours can be thwarted,
and that *in all things you are doing good,*
acting wisely and lovingly in the lives of your children.
Keep us in peace, accepting what lot you have for us.
Grant us submissive hearts under your loving hand.
Teach us to watch and wait for your final and holy purpose in all things.
Because we are recipients of abounding grace, may we rejoice even when
present circumstances bring us to tears.
You are utterly trustworthy!

✝ Amen.

Galatians 4:6; Colossians 1:21; 2 Corinthians 5:17; Mark 7:37; Job 1:21; 1 Samuel 2:7; Ephesians 1:11; Romans 8:28; Isaiah 26:3

OCTOBER

Does anyone have the foggiest idea what sort of power
we so blithely invoke?

ANNIE DILLARD

Father God, eternal God, God of peace,
Who *brought again from the dead our Lord Jesus,*
the Great Shepherd of the sheep, the guardian of our souls, we confess:
Other refuge have I none;
Hangs my helpless soul on thee.

Lord, I feel like I am hanging on by my fingernails . . .
This situation—which you know all about—seems so precarious.
I have many anxieties—they overwhelm me.
The future, the unknown, health issues,
money pressures, relationships—
something always seems to be going wrong.
Lord, Good Shepherd, I confess my anxieties are stronger than my trust.
Leave, ah, leave me not alone,
Still support and comfort me.
I find comfort in the assurance that *you care for the homeless, the penniless,*
the destitute, the widow.
You alone, O God, can turn our disasters into triumphs.
May we today, by your grace, be **triumphant** in our trials.

We have come to the *house of prayer*—
give ear, Lord, to our heart cry.
We have come to the house of praise—
awaken in us a thankful heart.
We have come to the house of godly instruction—
give your blessing to the Word preached.

May all who have *ears to hear* rejoice in the proclamation of God's truth.
Enlighten the ignorant,
awaken the careless,
reclaim the wandering,
establish the weak,
comfort the tested,
heal the afflicted.
Make ready a people for yourself, Lord.

You have forgiven our iniquities,
you have redeemed our lives from destruction,
you have crowned us with loving-kindness and tender mercies,
you have satisfied us with good things,
you have watched over us with more than maternal love.
We bless your holy name forever.

☦ 𝔄men.

Hebrews 13:20, KJV; Charles Wesley, "Jesus, Lover of My Soul"; Deuteronomy 10:17-18; Isaiah 56:7; Mark 4:23; Luke 1:17

Ramadan Prayer

Almighty and ever loving Father,
Whose mercies are without number,
  whose grace is without measure,
  whose purposes can never be thwarted,
we bow before you in humble recognition that you are
  the divine proprietor,
  the administrator of the affairs of men—
  indeed the whole world, the universe.
Your absolute sovereignty over all things is our conviction . . .
  but Lord we confess that often we are frustrated by your seeming
    inactivity.
We feel the pressure of the moment,
  the circumstances that need changing now,
  and we are sorely tempted to do something—
  to take matters into our own hands—instead of waiting on you.

Help us, Lord, not to be as King Saul who did not wait for a word from you,
  but tragically took matters into his own hands.
    Help us to wait upon you.
    Wait . . . wait . . . wait.
It took years before Naomi's heart turned toward Bethlehem.
  But all the while you were working on her behalf.
    Help us to wait on you.
    Wait . . . wait . . . wait.

In the fullness of time, God brought forth his Son . . .
    and that "fullness of time" was preceded by centuries
        of divine preparation.
Help us to wait . . . wait . . . wait.
Forgive us the sin of impatience.
For you have told us through the prophet Isaiah that
    you hear and understand our case,
    and you promise to give power to those who are tired and worn out,
    and you offer strength to the weak.
Once again we bring our unanswered prayers to you and the situations that
        seem irresolvable, unless you act . . .
    We try to leave it all with you.
    Help us to wait . . . wait . . . wait.

It is your nature, O God, to love . . . to love people who are troubled.
May all who are troubled this day see the hand of God at work in their lives.
    Have mercy on those who are brokenhearted.
    Forgive those who have fallen.
    Refresh those who are exhausted.
    May the *joy of the Lord* be their portion.

In the Muslim world, it is the time of Ramadan—daylight fasting.
We pray that you will lift the shroud of darkness covering countless Muslims:
    open their eyes of faith to see
    the *once-for-all sufficient, perfect, complete sacrifice for sin*
        in the death of Jesus Christ on the cross.
Protect and enable your witnesses to the gospel in those lands and
    send forth more laborers to the harvest,
remembering that
    you have appointed a day when the kingdoms of this world
    shall become the kingdoms of our Lord and he shall reign forever and ever.
Praise God!

With such victory ahead of us, we pray joyfully the prayer you taught the
disciples to pray:
Our Father which art in heaven,
hallowed be thy name.
Thy kingdom come,
thy will be done in earth,
as it is in heaven.
Give us this day our daily bread.
And forgive us our debts,
as we forgive our debtors.
And lead us not into temptation,
but deliver us from evil.
For thine is the kingdom, and the power, and the glory, for ever.

✝ Amen.

Luke 1:57; Isaiah 40:27-29; Nehemiah 8:10; Hebrews 10:12; Matthew 9:38;
Revelation 11:15; Matthew 6:9-13, KJV

Heavenly Father, blessed Son, eternal Spirit,
We worship you, our one God in three persons.
    Father, you have *loved us and sent Jesus Christ to redeem us.*
    Son of Righteousness, you *shed your own blood* to wash away our sins.
    Holy Spirit, you have *implanted in us eternal life* and revealed to us the
        glories of Jesus.
Since we are now in the care of the Great Shepherd,
    we are no longer in conflict with ourselves, with others, and with God.
We do want to *love you with all our heart, soul, and mind.*
But Lord, the suffering in the world is so widespread
    and the pain so great
        and the human carnage so terrible!
Many cannot trust the wisdom and power and goodness of Christ.
We confess that great mysteries surround the workings of God in this
    fallen creation.
We seek comforting answers but are often confounded at life's unanswerables.
    Help us, Lord!
Incline our hearts to trust your Word and its assurances
    that *you work all things according to the counsel of your will*
    and that *no purpose of yours can be thwarted.*
        We confess our wavering trust.
Let us hear again the good news that you *do all things well,*
    and in hearing . . . believe, trust, rejoice.
With you, Jesus, there is plenteous redemption.

So we thank you that our sins are forgiven
  and *remembered against us no more*.

This is a day of *glad tidings* . . .
  so we pray, God, that you will send additional laborers
    into the whitened harvest fields with the word of the gospel.
Bless, protect, and encourage your servants
  who have gone into hard fields and resistant places
    to *proclaim the message of salvation*.
Empower them with your Holy Spirit.
Enrich them with heavenly grace.
Protect them from the hatred of the evil one and his wicked emissaries.
Prosper your servants in their gospel efforts—
  give them many responsive souls.

Gracious God, remember in mercy the needs of this body.
  Comfort the grieving.
  Give peace to the struggling.
  Envelop the brokenhearted with your love.
  Give direction to those who don't know what to do.
  Provide divine strength to the tempted.
    Only you can meet the needs of your people, and we praise you.

And now, Father, we pray the prayer that Jesus taught his disciples to pray:
Our Father which art in heaven,
hallowed be thy name.
Thy kingdom come,
thy will be done in earth,
  as it is in heaven.
Give us this day our daily bread.
And forgive us our debts,
  as we forgive our debtors.
And lead us not into temptation,

but deliver us from evil.
For thine is the kingdom, and the power, and the glory, for ever.

✦ *Amen.*

Galatians 3:13; Ephesians 2:13; Ephesians 1:13; Mark 12:30; Ephesians 1:11; Job 42:2, NASB; Mark 7:37; Jeremiah 31:34; Romans 10:15; Isaiah 52:7; Matthew 6:9-13, KJV

God who hears and answers prayer,
Occupy the throne of my heart; take full possession and reign
    supremely.
    I need to rest in your sovereignty.
Things happen that cause me to doubt
    and to think that you are not really in charge.
Life is difficult for many of us and monumentally difficult for some.
    Unexpected, unwanted reversals make us feel so angry, so helpless.
    Canceled contracts, broken promises, serious health issues—
        it seems our anxieties are unremitting,
        our disappointments so devastating,
        family tragedies so cruel.
Our failures are so haunting, our past sins so condemnatory—
    we feel utterly helpless and can't help wondering,
        Why, God? Why?

The psalmist prayed, "*I will sing unto the Lord*
    because he has been so good to me."
We are staggered when we really grasp it: *You work for our good!*
Help us, Lord Jesus, to hold tenaciously to the truth
    that you can and will work all things for our good.
You do this that we might trust and depend upon you alone.
    You desire to *make us beautiful in your time.*
    Trust is beautiful . . . doubt is ugly.
        Beautiful Savior, make us beautiful.

Until we can see the present confused situation more clearly, we look back
over the years and we do see God's goodness in our lives.
Out of heartbreak, we do see good.
Out of despondency and confusion, we do see your goodness.
So we trust you today to bring us through what otherwise would
overwhelm us.
And so through all the length of days,
thy goodness faileth never.
Good Shepherd, may I sing thy praise
Within thy house forever.
Thanks be to God. Praise the Lord.
Our sins are forgiven,
our trust in you is renewed,
and we say as David did, in a dark hour of his life,
God is on my side!
Praise the Lord!

✝ Amen.

Psalm 13:6; Romans 8:28; Ecclesiastes 3:11; Henry Baker, "The King of Love My Shepherd Is";
Psalm 56:9, NLT

NOVEMBER

Abide in us, O strengthening Savior, to reinforce the faith by which
we may overcome the slumber of carnal security and, watching prayerfully,
resist evil forces which would keep us from Thee. O Jesus, without you
we can do nothing. Enrich our souls by the cleansing power of Thy blood.

WALTER A. MAIER

Veterans Day Prayer

Gracious God, eternal Father,
Who has *created us in your image*
    and *whose glory was revealed in the face of Jesus Christ,*
    give us insight to know Christ and his life,
        that the *same mind* which was in him may be in us.
By your abundant mercy,
    we have been born anew to a living hope
    through the resurrection of Jesus Christ from the dead
    to an inheritance which is imperishable, undefiled, and unfading,
    kept in heaven for us . . . where neither rust can corrupt
    nor thieves break in and steal.
We praise you for such redemption.
You rescued us from the *broad road that leads to destruction*
    and turned our hearts toward the narrow path that leads heavenward.
Though heaven is our home, we don't always manifest a heavenly spirit.
    For such failures in speech, attitudes, and actions,
        we fervently ask for your forgiveness.

{ SILENT PRAYER }

Thank you, Father, for forgiveness full and free.
Now may we heed the Lord's words, *"Go and sin no more."*

Lord Jesus, we have many needs,

needs greater than our ability to alleviate—but they are no challenge
    to you.
This day, this hour, may you provide, out of your abundance, sustaining
    grace to
    the grieving, the lonely, the financially burdened,
    the unemployed, those who suffer broken relationships,
    those in troubling circumstances,
    those facing secret battles against almost overwhelming temptations.
O God, you are able—we believe! Meet us in our needs today.
For those facing debilitating health issues—
    Lord, have mercy and grant them a healing touch.

Father God, we thank you for those of yesteryear
    who left home and family to defend our country.
        We enjoy the fruit of their sacrifice—we worship you in freedom.
Remember those of our extended family serving in the military.
    Keep them from hurt and destruction.
    Shield them from all harm.
    Work mightily in every heart, fulfilling your redemptive purposes.
    Enable those who believe to boldly and faithfully live a Christian
        life and may their testimony before fellow soldiers bear
        eternal fruit.
We pray for your return, meanwhile praying the prayer that Jesus taught
    his disciples to pray:
Our Father which art in heaven,
hallowed be thy name.
Thy kingdom come,
thy will be done in earth,
    as it is in heaven.
Give us this day our daily bread.
And forgive us our debts,
    as we forgive our debtors.

And lead us not into temptation,
but deliver us from evil.
For thine is the kingdom, and the power, and the glory, for ever.

✝ 𝕬men.

Genesis 1:27; 2 Corinthians 4:6; 1 Peter 4:1; 1 Peter 1:3-4, RSV; Matthew 6:20, KJV; Matthew 7:13; John 8:11; Matthew 6:9-13, KJV

Almighty God, magnanimous God,
We acknowledge you as Creator and sustainer of all things.
We praise you that you are not an absentee landlord,
  uninvolved in your creation,
    for you have promised that with regularity we shall experience
    summer and winter, seedtime and harvest.
The bounty of earth's produce at harvesttime
  should bring praise from mankind everywhere . . .
    and if many won't—we will.
We praise you for the provisions of life.

Blessed Savior, when we reflect on our past days,
  we see in every circumstance your providential hand—always offered
    in love.
So whatever difficulty we currently face, *we give you thanks.*
Thank you that you can turn the disappointments of life
  into divine purposefulness.
Consequently, even in our economic losses,
  our companionship losses,
  our experiential detours,
  our physical disruptions—
    we await your guiding hand, leading to our eternal benefit.

Good Shepherd, we thank you for your blessings upon your church.
We thank you for elders and pastors,

committed to the faithful declaration of the gospel—
both from this pulpit and missionary endeavors around the world.
We thank you for our worship facilities, with heat, light, and sound.
We thank you for adequate classroom space as well as areas for many other
activities.
We thank you for our custodial staff that keeps the house of God physically
inviting.
And so with your servant David, we pray:
I am overwhelmed by how much you have done for me.
I will tell everyone about your righteousness.
All day long I will proclaim your saving power.

✝ Amen.

Genesis 8:22; 1 Thessalonians 5:18; Psalm 71:15, NLT

Thanksgiving Prayer

Holy God, our Redeemer,
We give thanks to you, O God, for the goodness and love which you have
    made known to us in creation,
  in your Word spoken through the prophets,
  and in the Word made flesh, Jesus Christ,
    whom you sent to be the Savior and Redeemer of mankind.
In him you have delivered us from evil and have brought us
  out of error into truth,
  out of sin into righteousness,
    out of death into life.

Blessed Savior, when we reflect on our past days, we see in every
    circumstance your providential hand . . . always extended with love.
So whatever difficulty we currently face, we give you thanks.
  Thank you for protective shelter,
    sufficient food,
    adequate clothing,
    loving family,
    meaningful friendships.
All of these make our lives full, and we are grateful.
And so with your servant David we pray,
  "I am overwhelmed by how much you have done for me."

        ✝ *Amen.*

Psalm 71:15, NLT

Thanksgiving Prayer

Eternal God, our heavenly Father,
From whom comes *every good and perfect gift*,
we thank and praise your name for all your mercies,
    and for every blessing we have received from you.
We praise you, God, for health and strength,
    for food and raiment,
    for shelter, friends, and family,
    for comfort in sorrow, deliverance from danger,
    strength in weakness, help in adversity,
    consolation in affliction.
For all the tokens of your faithfulness,
    and for all the proofs of your mercy and love, we praise you.

We give you thanks, O God, for your Son, our Savior, Jesus Christ.
    No one in all history compares with him.
He is *the Good Shepherd*—
    the One who has guided us each step of the way.
He is *the Rock of Refuge*—
    the One who has held us securely when all around was sinking.
He is *the Bread of Life*—
    the One who has satisfied our soul's hunger.
He is *the Light of the World*—
    the One who has delivered us from spiritual darkness.
He is *the Resurrection*—
    the One who is our life here and our life to come.

So we praise you, Father, for bringing us to this place of spiritual refuge,
   a place where we hear the declaration of your Word.
Here the doors are open to any who would enter.
Here is a refuge, a sanctuary, a *balm in Gilead*,
   a resting place in *a weary land*, a grace-filled place
      where we all are *accepted in the Beloved*.
We thank you for every good deed done throughout our church family
   in the name of Christian love.
We praise you for the reality of the communion of the saints.

And so, Lord, for the supply of our needs and the preservation of our lives,
   for all the good you have bestowed upon us,
      and for all the evil you have averted,
we thank you, Father.
We praise you, O God.
We will *bless your holy name* forever and ever.

✝ *Amen.*

James 1:17; John 10:1-18; Psalm 71:3, NIV; John 6:35; John 8:12; John 11:25;
Jeremiah 8:22; Isaiah 32:2; Ephesians 1:6; Psalm 103:1

Almighty God, Father of all mercies,
We have been made aware of your bounty to us, even this past week
   as we enjoyed feasting and fellowship with our friends and loved ones.
We do give you thanks for all your **loving-kindness** to us.
So undeserving we are of your lavish gifts and boundless blessings.
May we show forth *praise—not only with our lips,* but in our lives—
   by walking before you in holiness and righteousness through Jesus Christ
      our Lord.

God of mercy, look with redemptive help upon desolate people living
   in places of calamity.
We pray for the victims of disaster—
   distraught, weary, homeless, sick, fearful, hungry, hurting.
      Spare the survivors from bitterness, despair, or fatalism.
Give wisdom to every relief worker,
   to all rescuers, doctors, nurses, dispensers of food and aid.
May their efforts be divinely blessed,
   opening numberless hearts to the gospel.
May your people in calamitous places—
   war-torn places,
   difficult places,
   spiritually desolate places—
be so graced by your provisions that
   many in spiritual darkness will see the light of the Lord Jesus Christ.

Great Shepherd, many in this congregation these days have faced *the roar of the lion.*
He prowls through the venue of sickness,
self-pity,
shattered relationships,
lust,
deception,
greener pastures,
failures of all kinds.
We would despair were it not for your promise of restoration.
For this we pray, right now.

{ SILENT PRAYER }

Again, thank you, Father.
Great peace have they who love your law,
and nothing can make them stumble.
We pray in the name of our Savior Jesus Christ who
is able to keep us from stumbling and to present us faultless
before the presence of his glory with exceeding joy.

✝ *Amen.*

Hebrews 13:15; John 8:12; 1 Peter 5:8; Psalm 119:165, NIV; Jude 1:24

DECEMBER

Although it is a day of great apostasy, yet it is apparently a day
of the wonderful works of God, wonders of power and mercy,
for He marvelously preserves His church and wants to be gracious to us
and make us monuments of His grace.

JONATHAN EDWARDS

Advent I

Sovereign Lord,
We thank you for being our *Wonderful Counselor, Mighty God,*
    Everlasting Father, and Prince of Peace.
In the fullness of time you, *the Word, became flesh and dwelt among us . . .*
    full of grace and truth.
Open our eyes to the great significance of the Incarnation, for you *have*
    visited and redeemed your people.
You have tented among us.
You have *come that we might have life!*
    O come, Thou Day-Spring,
        Come and cheer our spirits by thine advent here,
    And drive away the shades of night,
        And pierce the clouds and bring us light.

Yes, Lord, pierce the clouds that dim our trust in you:
    the clouds of grief,
    the clouds of loss,
    the clouds of disappointment,
    the clouds that make us wonder in our difficulties,
        Where are you?

O blessed Savior, light of my life,
    Holy Ghost, with light divine,
        Shine upon this heart of mine,
    Chase the shades of night away,
        Turn my darkness into day.

In doing this, Lord, I ask that you will enable me to henceforth *walk in the light.*

We pray for those who are serving you around the world, away from family, friends, and the fellowship of their church.
May the light of the gospel draw many in that place to a saving faith in our glorious God.
We ask your special blessing and presence today upon our pastor, enabling him to preach with clarity, unction, and earnestness,
as we open our hearts to the work of the Holy Spirit through the Word of God.

Sun of Righteousness, we do not yet know what we shall be,
but we do believe that when Jesus *shall appear, we shall be like him.*
So in between these two Advents,
may our longing,
our expectation,
our hope in him
make us pure even as he is pure.
We pray in Jesus' name.

✢ 𝔄men.

Isaiah 9:6; John 1:14; Luke 1:68; John 10:10, KJV; John Mason Neale,
"O Come, O Come, Emmanuel"; Andrew Reed, "Holy Ghost, with
Light Divine"; 1 John 1:7; Malachi 4:2; 1 John 3:2, KJV

Advent II

God of glory, God of light,
God of involvement in our predicament,
we praise you for your invasion into this fallen world—
   this place of deep darkness,
   this place of inexcusable rejection and unbelief.
You came, and you were not welcomed.
   But *the darkness can never extinguish the Light*!
   Praise your mighty name.
The light of the gospel has penetrated our darkened minds.
And now we see with holy appreciation some things surrounding your
      incarnation.
   Father God, we see your presence overshadowing
      the arrival of the wise men to worship Jesus.
   We see your presence with the angelic chorus,
      in the joyful shepherds,
      in the contemplative parents,
      in the beautiful baby.
But it is difficult to imagine your overshadowing presence in the soldiers'
      appearance at Bethlehem.
It is in the midst of tragedy, pain, and heartache that we imagine you are
      absent.
This is really self-centeredness, shortsightedness,
   to think that you don't care—
   that you have left us in the tough spots of life.

Isaiah makes it clear: the promised Savior will
bind up the brokenhearted,
comfort those who mourn,
give a crown of beauty for ashes,
give the garment of praise for the spirit of heaviness.
That is your promise for each of us today.
Help us to grasp it,
appropriate it,
be changed by it,
praise God for it.
So we do praise you that what you have promised you have fulfilled.
You have come to put away our sins . . . to utterly remove them from us
as far as the east is from the west.
Do so for each of us just now.

{ SILENT PRAYER }

Thank you, Father, gracious Savior, blessed Holy Spirit.

✣ *Amen.*

John 1:5, NLT; Isaiah 61:1-3, KJV, NLT; Psalm 103:12

Advent III

Our Father and our God,
We thank you for your *unspeakable gift*—
   the priceless gift—
   the unique gift—
   the matchless gift of your love, the baby of Bethlehem.
We do not worship a story.
We bow before a Sovereign: God clothed in human flesh.
The Creator has revealed himself to his creation, and we respond in praise.
As we contemplate the story of Christ's birth, we are arrested by the
      determined obedience of those involved.
   We hear Mary say, *"I am the Lord's servant. May everything you say about
      me come true."*
   We note the wise men: faithfully following the light they were given.
   We see the shepherds: hurriedly following the directions given by angels.
   We marvel at Joseph: leaving immediately for Egypt when he was
      warned in a dream.
Lord, we know you are pleased with joyful obedience.
Why are we so prone to neglect, ignore, delay, refuse, excuse, rebel against
      your clear commands?
   We know how we should live—why don't we?
   We know how we should treat one another—why don't we?
   We know how we should talk and act—why don't we?

Those obedient ones in Holy Scriptures convict us of our stubborn
      willfulness.

We confess our rebellion against your absolute, sovereign lordship,
   and ask that you would create in us a deep desire for you to rule over us.
Enable us to delight in this little child who is now the King of kings.
Help us to show our love for him through our obedience.
Amidst the lullabies of Christmas, may we hear Jesus say,
   "If you love me, keep my commandments."
Of all the things we might do this Christmastide,
   may we first and foremost love you supremely and obey you completely.
      Remove from our hearts any resistance to these desires.
We pray this in the powerful name of Jesus.

✢ *Amen.*

---

2 Corinthians 9:15, KJV; Luke 1:38, NLT; John 14:15

Advent IV

Glorious God, divine visitor, perfect promise keeper,
We echo the exultation of Zechariah, who praised the Lord because
   he *visited and redeemed his people*.
A mighty Savior has arrived, just as was promised through the holy
   prophets long ago.
That is the great Christmas evangel—*God fulfills his promises!*
We praise you, God, that you always keep your promises.
   And now we have *salvation through forgiveness of our sins*.
Praise God that light from heaven has penetrated this world's darkness.
Now, the redeemed can serve you, without fear,
   in holiness and righteousness, all our days.
So we praise you, God, with our lips.
We praise you in obedient living.
We praise you in a walk by faith.

Give me the faith of Mary, the confidence that *with God nothing will be
   impossible*.
   The Word of God cannot fail.
Let it be the cause of my rejoicing, that unto me, a Savior has been born.
   I needed a Savior—and am included in the angelic announcement:
      Unto you is born this day a Savior.
      Immanuel—"God with us"—
What a wonder to be a part of God's plan!

To know that we belong to you helps us not to fear . . .
Even so, dismiss my fears
    even as the shepherds of Bethlehem were told to dismiss their fears.
Father God, I confess that fears would grip me . . .
    fears of troubled times, financial pressures, uncertainties,
    deteriorating health, unemployment,
    calamitous family situations, unfulfilled expectations, aloneness.

To know that you have called us—
    Come to me, all of you who are weary and carry heavy burdens—
to know that you have called us
    helps us realize that you love us wherever we are.
Thank you, Father, for this unshakable truth.
Just now, make this truth real in every fearful heart, we pray.

✝ *Amen.*

Luke 1:68; 2 Chronicles 6:4, NIV; Luke 1:77, NLT; Luke 1:37; Luke 2:11, KJV;
Matthew 1:23; Matthew 11:28, NLT

Christmas Eve Prayer

Wonderful Counselor, Mighty God, Everlasting Father,
Prince of Peace,
These divinely given titles only partially describe you, baby of Bethlehem.
They cause us to stop—and worship you in wonder and adoration.
No typical baby, you:
You are a matchless gift from the eternal Kingdom.

Wonderful Counselor, we turn to you amidst the complexities of life, for your
counsel is sure.
You know all things—the beginning from the end;
with you is no darkness at all, no confusion, no contingencies.
We commit our needs, our way, our life to you—
direct us, Wonderful Counselor.

We turn to you, *Mighty God,* for we are limited.
In fact, everything we need comes from you.
Your *hand is not shortened,* not withered,
your thoughts are not clouded,
your purposes are never frustrated.
Nothing less than a Mighty God could reach us,
save us,
keep us,
provide for us,
raise us up in the last day,
where *we will be with the Lord forever.*

We turn to you, *Everlasting Father*, Holy Father,
   whose care for his children will never be eclipsed.
For some, the picture of a father's care is gravely distorted,
   but there is no disappointment with Jesus.
He alone can promise: *Cast all your care upon me, for I care for you.*
   Not just a few cares, not just for today,
      but all our cares—forever . . . Everlasting Father.

We turn to you, *Prince of Peace*, as the only one who can bring peace
   to our hearts, our homes,
   our cities, our country,
   our world.
Unregenerate mankind plots against God and his Anointed One,
   but their hideous rebellion shall utterly fail.
Someday—perhaps today—the Prince of Peace will come and make wars
      to cease:
   no more hatred, no more fighting, no more spilling of blood.
Then, not only wise men and shepherds will bow and worship,
   but the whole world—*every knee*—*will bow*
   and acknowledge him as the King of kings, Prince of Peace.
Even so, come, Lord Jesus!

✣ 𝔄men.

Isaiah 9:6, NLT; 1 John 1:5; Isaiah 59:1; 1 Thessalonians 4:17, NLT; 1 Peter 5:7;
Philippians 2:10, NASB; Revelation 22:20

Christmas Eve Prayer

Jesus, God of all our hopes,
We thank you for being
  our *Wonderful Counselor*—
    we need you to show us the way;
  our *Mighty God*—
    we need you to protect us from all evil;
  our *Everlasting Father*—
    we need the comfort of being in your family;
  our *Prince of Peace*—
    we need your peace in a troubled world.

Give us grace that we may seek *the way, the truth, and the life.*
Without you, we would wander off course—*broad is the way that leads
    to destruction.*
Without you, we would embrace error and *walk in darkness.*
Without you, we would remain in our sins and never know eternal life.
We praise you, that you have come so that we might *have life and have it
    abundantly.*
Just as you sent your messengers, the prophets, *to prepare the way* of salvation,
    may we prepare traditions that nurture our spiritual lives
    and celebrate the dawning of your everlasting Kingdom.
        Heaven and earth await that great event.
Even so, come, Lord Jesus!

                                    ✟ *Amen.*

Isaiah 9:6, NLT; John 14:6; Matthew 7:13; 1 John 1:6; John 10:10, NASB;
Isaiah 40:3; Revelation 22:20

New Year's Prayer

Glorious and covenant-keeping God,
By your grace we have reached another marker on our pilgrim journey.
Our times are in your hands, and we have come to this hour and this
 place by your mercies and by your grace.
We echo Jacob's words:
 God has been my shepherd all my life, his angel has kept me from all harm.
And those of Joshua:
 Every promise of the Lord has come true. Not a single one has failed!
Isaiah wrote:
 *I am overwhelmed with joy in the Lord my God! For he has dressed me with
 the clothing of salvation and draped me in a robe of righteousness.*
Jeremiah testifies:
 *Your words are what sustained me. They brought me great joy and are my
 heart's delight.*
Nahum tells us:
 The Lord is good. When trouble comes, he is a strong refuge.
Habakkuk recalls:
 The sovereign Lord is my strength!
Strength, shield, refuge, sustenance—sufficient promises for life's journey!
 Your Word, O Lord, assures us this is so.

We enjoy the privileges of grace because we have been reconciled
 to you.

There is therefore now no condemnation to them which are
in Christ Jesus.
May your grace, wonderful Savior, enable us to forget those things
that are *forgiven and held against us no more.*
Help us to let go of what you have forgiven and forgotten.

{ SILENT PRAYER }

Not only does your Word assure us of forgiveness, but we need not fear
the future.
You have told your people:
I know the thoughts that I think toward you, thoughts of peace and not disaster,
to give you a future and a hope.

So we commit ourselves anew to your gracious care and keeping in the
days ahead.
Whatever comes to us in the year ahead,
we believe *you alone do all things well.*
Since you are my Shepherd . . . *I shall not want.*
Father God, as I examine my wants, help me not to want anything you
won't give.
And Father God, give me grace to receive all that you give me this year.
We lift up our hearts in hope and trust toward you.
We believe your Word and rejoice in your promises.
Blessed be the glorious name of the Lord!

✢ *Amen.*

Genesis 48:15-16, NLT; Joshua 23:14, NLT; Isaiah 61:10, NLT; Jeremiah 15:16, NLT;
Nahum 1:7, NLT; Habakkuk 3:19, NLT; Romans 8:1, KJV; Hebrews 10:17;
Jeremiah 29:11; Mark 7:37; Psalm 23:1; Nehemiah 9:5

New Year's Prayer

God of the pilgrim's journey,
We lift up our souls in your presence,
  for your mercy endures forever, and your *compassions fail not*.
Holy Father, we come to the close of yet another year—now history,
    now only in our memory.
We have some regrets, many failures, things we wish we had done and
    said differently,
  ill feelings we held against those who meant us no harm,
  secret sins we nursed,
      inexcusable attitudes we excused.

We confess our sins to you and ask for forgiveness,
  believing that *as far as the east is from the west*
    you will remove our transgressions from us.
May your grace enable us to forget those things
  that are forgiven and held against us no more.

Father God, the new year lies before us, its events unknown to us—
    but not to you.
Hopes we cherish may be dashed,
  suffering may be at our door,
    disappointments may cloud our view of you.
If such be our lot, we will wait for your assurance that "all is well."
The days ahead may bring new friendships,

pleasant times,
spiritual victories,
    opportunities to help someone in need.
If this be our lot, may we be found as *faithful stewards.*

Sovereign Lord, amid the changing of our days, baptize us with the grace
    of appreciation.
Enlarge our capacity for joy.
Open our eyes to your work of grace all around us,
    in friendships and in the natural beauty of your creation;
    in books, and music, and art;
    in family life and in daily tasks.
May we sense your hand upon us.
May we grow happier as we grow older.

Lift up our hearts in hope and trust toward you.
We believe your Word and rejoice in your promises.
We commit ourselves anew
    to your gracious care and keeping in the days ahead.
We revel in the *peace that the world cannot give* or take away.
Blessed be the name of the Lord—
    the Alpha and the Omega, the Beginning and the End.

✣ *Amen.*

Lamentations 3:22; Psalm 103:12; 1 Corinthians 4:1-2; John 14:27, NLT; Revelation 22:13

PRAYERS FOR SPECIAL OCCASIONS

For everything there is a season,

a time for every activity under heaven.

A time to be born and a time to die.

A time to cry and a time to laugh.

A time to grieve and a time to dance.

THE PREACHER, ECCLESIASTES

Prayer for a New Pastor

Sovereign Lord,
We earnestly pray that you will superintend your servant to whom the
care of the souls of this congregation is now committed.
Grant that the Holy Spirit will prosper his shepherding,
that by his life and preaching
he may set forth your glory with all faithfulness.
Bless him in full measure with the gifts of the Holy Spirit
that he may truly and effectively declare the whole counsel of God,
to the end that sinners will learn the way of salvation
and your people will grow in holiness and righteous living.
May he always enter the pulpit with his own heart warned and warmed
by the truth he would declare.

Blessed Jesus, grant that this, your servant, whom you have called
and gifted,
be given a holy love for all of your people of this flock,
Give him great grace and zeal to shepherd us—
in our work and in our play,
in our joys and in our sorrows,
in our fears and in our hopes,
in our failures and in our successes.
In all things and at all times may he manifest the spirit of our Savior who
alone shall receive the preeminence.

Make his ministry here long and fruitful and the means of awakening
   the careless,
of comforting the afflicted,
and edifying the whole church,
   that we may experience the unity of the Spirit in the bond of love.
Guard him against the snares of the enemy:
   May he be kept pure in heart.
Grant, Holy Father, that he will receive the crown of life,
   which you have promised to your faithful ones.
Through Jesus Christ our Lord.

✢ *Amen.*

Church Business Meeting Prayer

Sovereign Lord, Great Shepherd of the sheep,
Meet with us this evening.
We recognize you as *head of the church*, which you *purchased with your own blood.*
We gather in no other name but yours.
We acknowledge no other leader but you.
You have blessed us in the past with godly leaders who loved us,
    cared for us,
    prayed for us,
    instructed us,
    lived righteously before us.
We praise you for every one of them, your faithful servants.

It is by your grace that we have come to this occasion.
We have prayed, and you have brought together the events
    of these days.
May we, like those praying believers in the book of Acts, be able to say,
    "It seemed good to the Holy Spirit, and to us."
    Lead us as you led the early church.
Now we earnestly seek your face in our deliberations.
As you led the Jerusalem Council,
    as you led the circle of believers at Antioch,
        lead us by giving us a spirit of unity.
However you lead us, God, may it be said of our church,
    "How they *love one another.*"

May your divine love permeate this place, now and always. We pray earnestly, believingly, in Jesus' name!

✝ *Amen.*

Colossians 1:18, NLT; Revelation 5:9, NIV; Acts 15:28; 1 John 4:12, NIV

Missions Sunday Prayer

Eternal God, God of creation, God of light and life,
We rejoice that *you are the same* . . . *yesterday, today, forever.*
With you there is *no shadow* . . . nothing brighter than you.
In your presence there is no aging, no decay, no dissolution.
You alone uphold all things by the power of your Word and the might
    of your hand.
Nations rise and fall at your command and for your purposes.
    Economies flourish or fail by your decree.
    The seasons come and go sweetly or severely, as you so direct.
      O thou who changest not, abide with me.

We come to you in this hour to ask that you abide with us.
    We once were in darkness—and didn't know it.
    We once were lost—and didn't care.
    We once were ruled by sin—and thought we enjoyed it.
    We once were in total unbelief—and thought we were smart.

But then Jesus came—and bid the darkness flee.
    Then Jesus came—and found the lost sheep.
    Then Jesus came—and took away my sin.
    Then Jesus came—and Truth became my guide.
O Lord, stay with me lest I grow cold, indifferent, worldly, and lose
    my way.
I need you far more than impressive portfolios,
    wobbly securities, managerial success;

I need you in the complexities of changing situations.
O Thou who changest not, abide with me.

The world around us, and the world far from us, languishes in spiritual
darkness.
You have asked us to pray that you would *send forth labourers—*
those who would plant the seed,
those who would water the seed,
and those who would reap a harvest of souls.
Some stand before us who have done that, but the need is still so great!
We pray you will call from this congregation those who will go.
We pray you will speak to others who will partner with the laborers.
We pray that a mighty flourishing of whitened fields, ready for harvesting,
shall be the experience of your laborers, worldwide.
In spite of the tares, may the harvesting go unimpeded.
May the translation, publication, distribution, and reading of your Word
be greatly blessed by you in these tumultuous days.
May each of us have some vital part in these endeavors.
We pray this in *the name which is above every name*, the name of Jesus.

✟ *Amen.*

Hebrews 13:8; James 1:17; Henry Lyte, "Abide with Me"; Matthew 9:38, KJV; Philippians 2:9

Wedding Prayer

Gracious God,
Bless this man and woman
who come now to join in Christian marriage.
May they give their vows to each other in the strength and spirit of your
    steadfast love.
Let the promises of your Word and the blessing of your presence in their
    home be their daily portion.
  May they grow in hope,
  vision,
  trust,
  usefulness,
    and friendship all their days.
May their home be a haven for many, as well as a model of fidelity.
By your grace, enable them to be true disciples of Jesus Christ, in whose
    name we pray.

✢ *Amen.*

Wedding Prayer

Lord of love,

Bless this man and this woman as, mysteriously and wonderfully, they now
are pledged as one.

By the power of your Holy Spirit pour out the abundance of your blessing
upon this new home, now established in Christ Jesus.

Give them health, strength, and wisdom to provide for the necessities of
life, but let them not be so consumed with the getting that they are
overtaken by the cares of life.

Give them a great capacity for tenderness,
an unusual gift of understanding,
a willingness to overlook each other's weaknesses
and see each other's strengths.

Give them an ever-growing love and fidelity that overcomes the hazardous
terrain of life's journey.

Give them a faith in your purposes—so strong that they will trust you no
matter what the future holds.

May _____ and _____ experience the promise of God to
Abraham,

I will bless you . . . and you shall be a blessing.

May all who enter their home leave spiritually enriched and blessed.

Thank you, heavenly Father, for your presence here with us and for your
promised blessing upon us, all the days of our lives.

✝ *Amen.*

Genesis 12:2

Funeral Prayer

Almighty and sovereign Lord of the universe,
We are assembled to acknowledge that *the breath of the Almighty gave life.*
You sustained it, and now you have taken it away.
 We await the glory of the Resurrection.
May your presence comfort those who mourn
 and those whose minds are filled with memories of past days.
  May they find peace in your all-wise providence.
Give us ears to hear your Words,
 Come to Me, all you who labor and are heavy laden, and I will give you rest.
We pray this in the name of Jesus, our victorious Lord and Savior.

✢ Amen.

Job 33:4; Matthew 11:28

Funeral Prayer

Almighty God and Sovereign of the universe,
We are assembled to acknowledge that you gave life—
　　you sustained it, and now you have taken it away.
　　　We await the glory of the Resurrection.
Illumine every heart with the light and hope of the gospel.
Scatter the shadows of sorrow, fear, unbelief.

Because of our Lord's glorious resurrection, we now rejoice that
　　they *who have fallen asleep* in Christ are not perished . . .
　　but being *absent from the body are present with the Lord* . . .
　　　in that city *whose builder and maker is God.*
This was the Bible-based conviction of _____, and is ours, too,
　　that you have *prepared a place for us,*
　　and you will come again,
　　　and *we will be with the Lord forever.*

No eye has seen, nor ear has heard,
no mind has conceived what you have prepared for those who love you,
　　into which glorious inheritance _____ has already entered.
Because this is true, we are triumphant even in the face of death.
Bless God for such victory.

　　　　　　　　　　　　　　　　　　　　　✝ **Amen.**

---

1 Thessalonians 4:13; 2 Corinthians 5:8; Hebrews 11:10; John 14:2; 1 Thessalonians 4:17, NIV;
1 Corinthians 2:9, NIV.

Memorial Service Prayer

Sovereign God,
Fill our minds with grandeur at the thought
    that with you *one day is as a thousand years,*
    and a thousand years as one day.
We see change and decay all around,
    yet with you there is *no variableness, neither shadow of turning,*
    rather, glorious immortality.

May we rejoice that while men die . . . *the Lord lives!*
That while all creatures are broken reeds,
    empty cisterns,
    fading flowers,
    withering grass,
You, O Lord, are the Rock of Ages,
    the fountain of *living water,*
    the joy of man's desiring,
        the giver of rest to the contrite heart.

                                  ✝ *Amen.*

---

2 Peter 3:8; James 1:17, KJV; Psalm 18:46; John 7:38

Memorial Service Prayer

Almighty God,
Who *knows our frame and remembers that we are dust,*
   look in your great compassion upon us
   who have been brought into the presence of sorrow
      and under the dark *shadow of death.*

You are no stranger to a household experiencing great loss:
For *you wept* at the grave of Lazarus
      and reminded Mary and Martha of the truth of the Resurrection
         and life to come.
As you comforted them, comfort us.
Speak to us of eternal things,
   and when our spirits sink
      before the mystery of life and of death, assure us that
      Neither death nor life . . . shall be able to separate us from the love of God
         which is in Christ Jesus our Lord.

✝ *Amen.*

Psalm 103:14; Psalm 23:4; John 11:35; Romans 8:38-40

Memorial Service Prayer

Blessed Redeemer—great Balm in Gilead,
We worship you, the victor over all that would defeat us.
If we didn't know you, we would be utterly crushed in this hour.
If we didn't believe you were *touched with the feeling of our infirmities*—
    we would be comfortless.
If we didn't believe your eternal Word, we would be filled with despair.
But thanks be to God—we are not overcome but rather,
  by the blood of the Lamb,
    we are overcomers.
Bless God forever.

Lord, we have sung many times "Let the Beauty of Jesus Be Seen in Me"—
    but seldom have we witnessed the Lord's beauty as we did in the life
    of your child, _____.
Your child's journey was not a flower-strewn pathway . . . but rather, one
    crushing experience after another—out of which comes the fragrance
    only Christ can give.
Our friend faced the crucible with joyful exuberance.
  May God's beauty rest upon the family—
    Beauty in every coming adjustment, in every difficult decision,
experiencing day by day God's promised provision:
  As your days, so shall your strength be.
This we pray in the beautiful name of Jesus.

                                 ☦ Amen.

Hebrews 4:15, KJV; Deuteronomy 33:25

Graveside Prayer

Almighty God,
We come to you, the Lord of life.
You have conquered death and because you arose from the dead,
  we have the assurance that
    we, too, shall be resurrected.
This is our hope and this is our consolation in Christ Jesus.
Now, God of peace, go with us and give us peace.

✞ *Amen.*

PRAYER NUMBER SEVENTY-FOUR

My Own Prayer

My Own Prayer

TOPICAL INDEX BY PRAYER NUMBER

172